MW00679077

Pork

Easy · Delicious · Versatile

THE AUSTRALIAN
Women's Weekly

Welcome. It is our pleasure to bring you, in partnership with the Australian Women's Weekly, the very best of Pork recipes. Succulent, tender, nutritious and lean, you'll find Pork is versatile and easy to cook. We've scoured the world to collect these delicious, simple recipes for the whole family to enjoy. From quick and easy weekday dinners, to 'wow factor' weekend meals, this book is a must for every creative kitchen.

Australian Pork Limited

contents

starters

4

pork and prawn rolls

300g pork mince
500g cooked medium king prawns
1⅓ cups (80g) finely shredded iceberg lettuce
1 cup (80g) bean sprouts
½ cup loosely packed fresh mint leaves
12 x 17cm-square rice paper sheets
hoisin peanut dipping sauce
2 teaspoons caster sugar
1 tablespoon rice vinegar
¼ cup (60ml) water
¼ cup (60ml) hoisin sauce
1 tablespoon crushed roasted peanuts

1 Cook pork, stirring, about 5 minutes, in heated oiled medium frying pan until browned lightly and cooked through.
2 Meanwhile, shell and devein prawns; chop prawn meat finely.
3 Make hoisin peanut dipping sauce.
4 Combine lettuce, sprouts and mint in medium bowl.

5 To assemble rolls, place 1 sheet of rice paper in medium bowl of warm water until just softened. Lift sheet from water carefully; place, with one point of the square sheet facing you, on board covered with tea towel. Place a little of the prawn meat vertically along centre of sheet; top with a little of the pork then a little of the lettuce filling. Fold top and bottom corners over filling then roll sheet from side to side to enclose filling. Repeat with remaining rice paper sheets, prawn meat, pork and lettuce filling.
6 Serve rolls with dipping sauce.
hoisin peanut dipping sauce Stir sugar, vinegar and the water in small saucepan over medium heat until sugar dissolves. Stir in sauce and nuts.

preparation time 25 minutes
cooking time 10 minutes makes 12
nutritional count per roll
1.6g total fat (0.3g saturated fat); 367kJ (87 cal); 6.1g carbohydrate; 11.3g protein; 1.3g fibre

crunchy pork noodle balls

1 bundle (60g) dried egg noodles
250g pork mince
1 small red onion (100g), chopped finely
2 cloves garlic, crushed
2 teaspoons grated fresh ginger
⅓ cup coarsely chopped fresh coriander
1 egg yolk
¼ cup (35g) plain flour
1 teaspoon sambal oelek
1 teaspoon fish sauce
peanut oil, for deep-frying
⅓ cup (80ml) sweet chilli sauce
2 tablespoons lime juice

1 Crumble noodles into a large heatproof bowl, cover with boiling water, stand about 5 minutes or until tender; drain.
2 Combine noodles with pork, onion, garlic, ginger, coriander, egg yolk, flour, sambal and fish sauce in large bowl. Roll rounded teaspoons of mixture into balls.
3 Heat oil in large saucepan; deep-fry pork balls, in batches, until browned and cooked through, drain on absorbent paper. Serve with combined sweet chilli sauce and juice.

preparation time 15 minutes
cooking time 5 minutes makes 36
nutritional count per noodle ball
0.7g total fat (0.1g saturated fat); 88kJ (21 cal);
2.5g carbohydrate; 0.9g protein; 0.3g fibre

pork dumplings

250g pork mince
½ cup (40g) finely chopped wombok
2 green onions, chopped finely
2 tablespoons finely chopped
    fresh garlic chives
2cm piece fresh ginger (10g), grated
2 teaspoons light soy sauce
2 teaspoons cornflour
40 wonton wrappers
dipping sauce
¼ cup (60ml) light soy sauce
2 teaspoons white vinegar
2 teaspoons brown sugar

1 Combine pork, wombok, onion, chives, ginger, sauce and cornflour in medium bowl.
2 Place 1 level teaspoon of the pork mixture into centre of each wonton wrapper; brush edges with a little water, pinch edges together to seal.
3 Place dumplings, in batches, in large baking-paper-lined bamboo steamer. Steam, covered, over large saucepan of boiling water about 4 minutes or until cooked through.
4 Meanwhile, combine ingredients for dipping sauce in small bowl.
5 Serve dumplings with dipping sauce.

preparation time 25 minutes
cooking time 15 minutes makes 40
nutritional count per dumpling
0.2g total fat (0g saturated fat); 63kJ (15 cal);
0.6g carbohydrate; 2.5g protein; 0g fibre

minestrone

2 smoked ham hocks (1kg)
1 medium brown onion (150g), quartered
1 trimmed celery stalk (100g),
    chopped coarsely
1 teaspoon black peppercorns
1 bay leaf
4 litres (16 cups) water
1 tablespoon olive oil
2 trimmed celery stalks (200g),
    chopped finely
1 large carrot (180g), chopped finely
3 cloves garlic, crushed
¼ cup (70g) tomato paste
2 large tomatoes (440g), chopped finely
1 small leek (200g), sliced thinly
1 cup (100g) small pasta shells
420g can white beans, rinsed, drained
½ cup coarsely chopped fresh
    flat-leaf parsley
½ cup coarsely chopped fresh basil
½ cup (40g) shaved parmesan cheese

1 Preheat oven to 220°C/200°C fan-forced.
2 Roast hocks and onion in baking dish, uncovered, 30 minutes. Combine with coarsely chopped celery, peppercorns, bay leaf and the water in large saucepan; bring to the boil. Simmer, uncovered, 2 hours.
3 Remove hocks from soup. Strain broth through muslin-lined sieve or colander into large heatproof bowl; discard solids. Allow broth to cool, cover; refrigerate until cold. When cool, remove ham from bones; shred coarsely. Discard bones.
4 Meanwhile, heat oil in large saucepan; cook finely chopped celery and carrot, stirring, 2 minutes. Add ham, garlic, paste and tomato; cook, stirring, 2 minutes.
5 Discard fat from surface of broth. Place broth in measuring jug; add enough water to make 2 litres. Add broth to pan; bring to the boil. Simmer, covered, 20 minutes.
6 Add leek, pasta and beans; bring to the boil. Simmer, uncovered, until pasta is just tender. Remove from heat; stir in herbs. Serve soup sprinkled with cheese.

preparation time 40 minutes (plus refrigeration time)
cooking time 3 hours 35 minutes serves 6
nutritional count per serving
7.2g total fat (2.4g saturated fat); 865kJ (207 cal);
19.6g carbohydrate; 12.7g protein; 6.1g fibre
tip You can make the broth either the day before or in the morning of the day you want to finish preparing the minestrone so that it chills long enough for the fat to solidify on top; skim it away before reheating the broth.

pork and vegetable wonton soup

3 litres (12 cups) water
1kg chicken bones
1 small brown onion (80g), quartered
1 medium carrot (120g), quartered
4cm piece fresh ginger (20g), grated
2 fresh small red thai chillies, halved
150g pork mince
1 clove garlic, crushed
1 green onion, chopped finely
2 tablespoons finely chopped
 water chestnuts
2 tablespoons finely chopped
 fresh coriander
1 teaspoon sesame oil
2 tablespoons chinese cooking wine
¼ cup (60ml) light soy sauce
2 teaspoons white sugar
12 wonton wrappers
1 cup firmly packed watercress sprigs
4 fresh shiitake mushrooms, sliced thinly

1 Place the water in large saucepan with bones, brown onion, carrot, three-quarters of the ginger and 2 chilli halves; bring to the boil. Reduce heat; simmer, covered, 2 hours.

2 Strain broth through muslin-lined sieve or colander into large heatproof bowl; discard solids. Allow broth to cool; cover, refrigerate.

3 Meanwhile, chop remaining chilli finely; combine in bowl with remaining ginger, pork, garlic, green onion, water chestnut, coriander, oil, 2 teaspoons of the wine and 1 teaspoon each of the sauce and the sugar.

4 Place 1 level tablespoon of filling in centre of each wonton wrapper; brush edges with a little water. Gather edges around filling; pinch together.

5 Skim and discard fat from surface of broth. Return broth to large saucepan with remaining wine, sauce and sugar; bring to the boil. Add wontons, reduce heat; cook, uncovered, about 5 minutes or until cooked.

6 Divide watercress, mushrooms and wontons among bowls; top with broth.

preparation time 40 minutes
cooking time 2 hours 10 minutes **serves** 4
nutritional count per serving
3.5g total fat (0.8g saturated fat); 585kJ (140 cal); 7.6g carbohydrate; 15.8g protein; 2.4g fibre
tip Use crisp, crunchy fresh water chestnuts for this recipe if they are in season; frozen fresh water chestnuts also can be found in many Asian grocers. You need to buy about 5 medium-sized chestnuts for this soup. Uncooked wontons can be frozen until required; cook, straight from the freezer, in the broth.

roasts & bakes

pork leg roast with sage potatoes

You can use boneless pork shoulder roast, if you like.

2.5kg boneless pork leg roast, rind on
2 tablespoons olive oil
1 tablespoon sea salt flakes
6 medium potatoes (1.2kg), quartered
2 tablespoons olive oil, extra
2 tablespoons fresh sage leaves
2 tablespoons fresh rosemary leaves
raspberry glaze
1 cup (320g) cranberry sauce
⅔ cup (100g) fresh or frozen raspberries
½ cup (110g) sugar
⅓ cup (80ml) balsamic vinegar

1 Preheat oven to 220°C/200°C fan-forced.
2 Score pork rind with sharp knife; rub with oil, then salt.
3 Place pork in large shallow baking dish. Roast, uncovered, 20 minutes.
4 Reduce oven to 180°C/160°C fan-forced. Roast, uncovered, about 2 hours.
5 Meanwhile, combine potato with extra oil, sage and rosemary in large bowl. Place in single layer on oven tray. Roast, uncovered, about 35 minutes.
6 Make raspberry glaze.
7 Stand pork covered loosely with foil 10 minutes before slicing. Serve pork and potatoes with raspberry glaze.
raspberry glaze Combine ingredients in medium saucepan; cook, stirring, over heat until sugar dissolves. Simmer, 15 minutes or until mixture is reduced by about half.

preparation time 20 minutes (plus standing time)
cooking time 2 hours 35 minutes serves 9
nutritional count per serving
30.2g total fat (8.6g saturated fat); 2851kJ (682 cal); 36.3g carbohydrate; 64g protein; 3.7g fibre

honey-glazed pork loin

Ask the butcher to remove the rind
completely from the pork loin and score it.

2.5kg boneless loin of pork
2 teaspoons vegetable oil
1 tablespoon sea salt flakes
2 cloves garlic, crushed
1 tablespoon finely chopped fresh sage
⅓ cup (90g) honey, warmed
1 tablespoon red wine vinegar
2 cups (500ml) chicken stock
2 tablespoons cornflour
2 tablespoons water

1 Preheat oven to 220°C/200°C fan-forced.
2 Place pork rind, fat-side down, on wire
rack in large shallow baking dish; rub
with oil, then salt. Roast, uncovered, about
30 minutes or until crackling is crisp and
browned; cool. Discard fat from dish.
3 Place pork, fat-side down, on board;
spread with half the combined garlic and
sage. Roll pork; secure with kitchen string
at 2cm intervals.

4 Place pork on wire rack in baking dish.
Reduce oven to 200°C/180°C fan-forced;
roast pork, uncovered, 30 minutes. Cover
pork with foil, reduce oven to 180°C/160°C
fan-forced; roast 1 hour.
5 Combine honey and vinegar with
remaining sage and garlic; brush pork with
half of the honey mixture. Roast pork,
uncovered, 30 minutes, brushing occasionally
with remaining honey mixture. Remove pork
from dish; cover with foil.
6 Meanwhile, strain pan juices from baking
dish into heatproof jug; remove fat from
juices (you will need ⅔ cup of juices). Add
stock to dish with juices. Stir in blended
cornflour and the water; stir until gravy
boils and thickens.
7 Serve pork slices with crackling and gravy.

preparation time 20 minutes
cooking time 2 hours 40 minutes serves 9
nutritional count per serving
5.7g total fat (1.6g saturated fat); 1471kJ (352 cal);
10.7g carbohydrate; 63.5g protein; 0.1g fibre

pork loin with fresh peach chutney

Ask the butcher to remove the rind
completely from the pork loin and score it.

2kg boneless loin of pork, rind off
1 tablespoon olive oil
½ teaspoon celery seeds
1 teaspoon sea salt flakes
fresh peach chutney
2 large peaches (440g), chopped coarsely
1 large brown onion (200g),
    chopped coarsely
¼ cup (40g) coarsely chopped raisins
2cm piece fresh ginger (10g), grated
1 cup (220g) white sugar
1 cup (250ml) cider vinegar
1 cinnamon stick
¼ teaspoon ground clove

1 Make fresh peach chutney.
2 Preheat oven to 200°C/180°C fan-forced.
3 Rub pork loin with half the oil; sprinkle
with seeds. Place pork on wire rack in large
shallow baking dish; roast, uncovered, about
1 hour. Place pork on heated plate, cover
loosely with foil.
4 Increase oven to 220°C/200°C fan-forced.
5 Remove excess fat from underside of rind;
rub rind with remaining oil then salt. Place
rind, fat-side down, on wire rack in shallow
baking dish; roast, uncovered, 15 minutes or
until crisp and browned.
6 Serve sliced pork and crackling with chutney.
fresh peach chutney Stir ingredients in
medium saucepan over heat, without boiling,
until sugar dissolves; bring to the boil. Reduce
heat; simmer, uncovered, stirring occasionally,
about 1¾ hours or until mixture thickens.
Discard cinnamon. Pour chutney into hot
sterilised jars, seal while hot.

preparation time 35 minutes
cooking time 3 hours serves 6
nutritional count per serving
8.5g total fat (2.1g saturated fat); 2429kJ (581 cal);
47.1g carbohydrate; 76.6g protein; 1.7g fibre
tip The chutney can be made up to 3 months ahead.
Store in a cool dark place. Refrigerate after opening.

pork.

It's got something for everyone.

The whole family will benefit from more Pork on the menu. It doesn't just taste great, it's also an excellent source of lean protein for growing bodies. In fact, Pork is so lean and nutritious, there are 15 cuts approved by the Heart Foundation.

Today it is even more important to find healthier meal options everyone can enjoy to help avoid the increase in both adult and children's obesity. A healthy weight is the result of healthy eating habits, not the outcome of miserable restrictive eating. Adding lean Pork cuts to your weekly family meals will help lessen the chance of over-consumption of high kilojoule fatty foods.

Cooking lean Pork is so easy, use medium heat and cook it until there's just a hint of pink. This produces a great taste even kids will love. Serve it with your favourite sauce, vegies, rice or pasta.

By adding Pork to your family's diet you will earn a tick in the healthy eating box. Pork is so much more than a special-occasion family roast. Try any Heart Foundation Tick-approved lean Pork cut, trimmed of visible fat – there's a cut for every day of the week.

Pork is so versatile. Try substituting Pork for other meat in your recipes – it makes great stir-fries, barbecues and roasts. Pork contains vitamins B6 for muscular growth, B12 for a healthy nervous system and thiamin, niacin and zinc for immunity.

It's always a good idea to vary your diet, so by incorporating Pork into your family's menu, you're treating them in more ways than one.

% Recommended daily intake (RDI) key nutrients in 150g serving of lean pork*.

Nutrient	RDI	% RDI
Protein (g)	45g	77%
Thiamin (mg)	1.1mg	136%
Riboflavin (mg)	1.72mg	10%
Niacin (mg)	10mg	139%
Pyridoxine B6 (mg)	1.6mg	50%
B12 (mcg)	2mcg	25%
Zinc (mg)	12mg	23%
Iron (mg)	12mg	9%
Selenium (mg)	70mg	43% Female RDI

*APL Nutrient Profile of Pork as purchased by consumers throughout Australia in 2005-06.
Study overseen by Associate Professor Dr H. Greenfield unpublished data.

150g serving of lean pork.

orange-glazed ham

6kg smoked leg of ham
2 small oranges (360g), halved, sliced thinly
1 tablespoon (6g) whole cloves
orange glaze
½ cup (170g) orange marmalade
¾ cup (180ml) orange juice
¼ cup (50g) firmly packed brown sugar
2 teaspoons dijon mustard
2 tablespoons Cointreau or Grand Marnier

1 Cut through ham rind about 10cm from the shank end of leg. Remove rind from ham by sliding your hand between the rind and the fat layer. Discard rind.
2 Preheat oven to 180°C/160°C fan-forced.
3 Make orange glaze.

4 Secure orange slices with cloves in decorative pattern on ham.
5 Wrap shank in foil; brush ham with some of the orange glaze. Roast ham, covered, brushing occasionally with more glaze, about 2 hours or until orange is lightly caramelised and ham is heated through.
orange glaze Stir ingredients in small saucepan over low heat until warm.

preparation time 40 minutes (plus cooling time)
cooking time 2 hours 45 minutes serves 15
nutritional count per serving
16.9g total fat (6.2g saturated fat); 1806kJ (432 cal); 14g carbohydrate; 54.4g protein; 0.5g fibre
tip If you like, or if your oven is busy, glaze the ham in the barbecue, using indirect heat, following manufacturer's instructions.

chinese barbecued spare ribs

¾ cup (180ml) barbecue sauce
2 tablespoons dark soy sauce
1 tablespoon honey
¼ cup (60ml) orange juice
2 tablespoons brown sugar
1 clove garlic, crushed
2cm piece fresh ginger (10g), grated
2kg american-style pork ribs

1 Combine sauces, honey, juice, sugar, garlic and ginger in large shallow baking dish; add ribs, turn to coat in marinade. Cover; refrigerate 3 hours or overnight.
2 Preheat oven to 180°C/160°C fan-forced.
3 Brush ribs both sides with marinade; roast, covered, 45 minutes. Uncover; roast about 15 minutes.

preparation time 15 minutes (plus refrigeration time)
cooking time 1 hour serves 4
nutritional count per serving
26.4g total fat (10.2g saturated fat); 2675kJ (640 cal); 35.2g carbohydrate; 64.7g protein; 0.8g fibre

roast loin of pork with balsamic glaze

Ask the butcher to roll the loin and score the rind finely for you.

2 sprigs fresh rosemary
2.5kg boneless loin of pork, rind on
1 tablespoon olive oil
1 tablespoon sea salt flakes
2 bunches (700g) spring onions
2 bulbs garlic
balsamic glaze
½ cup (125ml) balsamic vinegar
1⅓ cups (330ml) chicken stock
1 teaspoon cornflour
1 tablespoon water
10g butter

1 Preheat oven to 250°C/230°C fan-forced.
2 Tuck the rosemary into the string under the pork. Place the pork in a large baking dish. Rub the rind with oil then salt. Roast, uncovered, for about 40 minutes or until rind blisters. Drain excess fat from dish.
3 Meanwhile, trim onions, leaving 4cm long stems. Cut tops from garlic bulbs.
4 Reduce oven to 180°C/160°C fan-forced. Place onions and garlic in baking dish with pork. Roast about 1 hour or until pork is cooked through.
5 Transfer pork to heated plate; cover with foil, stand while making balsamic glaze. Drain juices from dish into a large heatproof jug; skim fat from top.
6 Serve pork with vegetables and glaze.
balsamic glaze Heat same baking dish on stove; add vinegar, simmer, uncovered, until syrupy and reduced to about 2 tablespoons. Whisk in stock, reserved pan juices with blended cornflour and the water. Stir until mixture boils and thickens slightly. Add butter, stir until melted. Strain glaze through a fine sieve.

preparation time 10 minutes
cooking time 1 hour 45 minutes serves 9
nutritional count per serving
23.6g total fat (8.2g saturated fat); 1956kJ (468 cal); 2.7g carbohydrate; 60.3g protein; 2.1g fibre

roasted pork fillet with pear and apricot relish

410g can sliced pears in natural juice
410g can apricot halves in natural juice
600g pork fillet
1 tablespoon olive oil
½ cup (125ml) water
2 tablespoons white wine vinegar
1 fresh long red chilli, chopped finely
¼ cup (40g) sultanas
2 tablespoons white sugar

1 Preheat oven to 220°C/200°C fan-forced.
2 Drain pears over small bowl. Reserve juice; chop pears coarsely. Drain apricots, discarding juice. Chop apricots coarsely.
3 Place pork in small shallow baking dish; drizzle with oil. Roast, uncovered, about 20 minutes or until cooked as desired. Cover loosely with foil; stand 5 minutes then slice thickly.
4 Meanwhile, place pear, apricot, reserved juice and remaining ingredients in medium saucepan; bring to the boil. Reduce heat; simmer, uncovered, about 20 minutes or until relish thickens slightly.
5 Serve pork with relish.

preparation time 10 minutes
cooking time 20 minutes serves 4
nutritional count per serving
7g total fat (1.4g saturated fat); 1379kJ (330 cal); 29.2g carbohydrate; 35.3g protein; 3.3g fibre

salt and pepper roast pork

1.2kg pork mini roast, rind on
1 tablespoon sea salt flakes
½ teaspoon dried chilli flakes
½ teaspoon rice flour
½ teaspoon cracked black pepper
2 tablespoons olive oil

1 Preheat oven to 220°C/200°C fan-forced.
2 Score pork rind with sharp knife.
3 Combine salt, chilli, flour and pepper in small bowl. Rub pork with oil; sprinkle with salt mixture. Roast, uncovered, 20 minutes.
4 Reduce oven to 180°C/160°C fan-forced. Roast, uncovered, about 1¼ hours.
5 Cover pork loosely with foil, stand 10 minutes before slicing thickly.

preparation time 10 minutes (plus standing time)
cooking time 1 hour 35 minutes serves 4
nutritional count per serving
49.6g total fat (15.1g saturated fat); 2859kJ (684 cal); 0.4g carbohydrate; 60g protein; 0.1g fibre

roasted pork belly with plum sauce

800g boneless pork belly, rind on
1 teaspoon vegetable oil
2 teaspoons sea salt flakes
1 cup (250ml) water
1½ cups (375ml) chicken stock
2 tablespoons dark soy sauce
¼ cup (60ml) chinese cooking wine
¼ cup (55g) firmly packed brown sugar
2 cloves garlic, sliced thinly
3cm piece fresh ginger (15g), sliced thinly
1 cinnamon stick, crushed
1 teaspoon dried chilli flakes
⅓ cup (80ml) orange juice
6 cloves
1 teaspoon fennel seeds
4 plums (450g), cut into eight wedges
cucumber salad
1 lebanese cucumber (130g)
1 fresh long green chilli, sliced thinly
⅔ cup coarsely chopped fresh mint
1 tablespoon vegetable oil
1 tablespoon lemon juice
1 teaspoon white sugar

1 Preheat oven to 180°C/160°C fan-forced.
2 Place pork on board, rind-side up. Using sharp knife, score rind by making shallow cuts diagonally in both directions at 3cm intervals; rub oil then salt into cuts.
3 Combine the water, stock, sauce, cooking wine, sugar, garlic, ginger, cinnamon, chilli, juice, cloves and seeds in large shallow baking dish. Place pork in dish, rind-side up; roast, uncovered, 1 hour 20 minutes. Increase oven to 220°C/200°C fan-forced. Roast pork, uncovered, about 15 minutes or until crackling is crisp.
4 Remove pork from dish to heated plate; cover loosely with foil. Strain liquid in baking dish into medium saucepan, skim away surface fat; bring to the boil. Add plums, reduce heat; simmer, uncovered, about 15 minutes or until plum sauce thickens.
5 Meanwhile, make cucumber salad.
6 Serve thickly sliced pork with plum sauce and salad.
cucumber salad Using vegetable peeler, cut cucumber lengthways into ribbons. Place cucumber in large bowl with remaining ingredients; toss gently to combine.

preparation time 20 minutes
cooking time 1 hour 55 minutes serves 4
nutritional count per serving
51g total fat (16.2g saturated fat); 3010kJ (720 cal); 25.6g carbohydrate; 39.1g protein; 3.4g fibre

slow-roasted pork with fennel

1.5kg pork scotch fillet
1 clove garlic, crushed
1 teaspoon fennel seeds
1 tablespoon olive oil
⅔ cup (160ml) dry white wine
⅓ cup (80ml) chicken stock
6 medium fennel bulbs (1.8kg),
    halved lengthways
80g butter, softened
3 cloves garlic, sliced thinly

1 Tie pork with kitchen string at 2cm intervals. Combine crushed garlic and seeds; rub over pork.
2 Preheat oven to 150°C/130°C fan-forced.
3 Heat oil in large flameproof baking dish; cook pork, uncovered, over heat until browned all over. Add wine and stock; bring to the boil. Cover dish tightly with foil or lid; roast in oven 1½ hours.
4 Add fennel to dish, dot with combined butter and sliced garlic; roast, covered, 1¼ hours, turning pork and fennel occasionally.
5 Increase oven to 200°C/180°C fan-forced.
6 Uncover pork, spoon pan juices over pork and fennel. Roast, uncovered, 20 minutes or until browned. Transfer pork and fennel to serving platter, cover loosely with foil; stand 15 minutes.
7 Meanwhile, place baking dish over heat; bring pan juices to the boil. Reduce heat; simmer, uncovered, until mixture reduces to about 2 cups. Pour pan juices over pork and fennel to serve.

preparation time 25 minutes
cooking time 3 hours 25 minutes (plus standing time)
serves 6
nutritional count per serving
34.2g total fat (14.4g saturated fat); 2412kJ (577 cal);
5.9g carbohydrate; 55.1g protein; 5.1g fibre

pork loin with spinach and pancetta stuffing

When you order the pork loin, ask the butcher to leave a tail measuring about 20cm in length with rind removed, to help make rolling the stuffed loin easier.

4 slices white bread (120g)
2 tablespoons olive oil
1 clove garlic, crushed
1 medium brown onion (150g),
    chopped coarsely
6 slices pancetta (90g), chopped coarsely
100g baby spinach leaves
¼ cup (35g) roasted macadamias,
    chopped coarsely
½ cup (125ml) chicken stock
2kg boneless loin of pork, rind on
plum and red wine sauce
1½ cups (480g) plum jam
2 tablespoons dry red wine
⅔ cup (160ml) chicken stock

1 Preheat oven to 200°C/180°C fan-forced.
2 Discard bread crusts; cut bread into 1cm cubes. Heat half of the oil in large frying pan; cook bread, stirring, until browned. Drain croutons on absorbent paper.
3 Heat remaining oil in same pan; cook garlic, onion and pancetta until onion browns lightly. Stir in spinach; remove from heat. Stir in croutons, nuts and stock.
4 Place pork on board, fat-side down; slice through thickest part of pork horizontally, without cutting through other side. Open out pork to form one large piece; press stuffing mixture against loin along width of pork. Roll pork to enclose stuffing, securing with kitchen string at 2cm intervals.
5 Place pork on wire rack in large shallow baking dish. Roast, uncovered, 1¼ hours or until cooked through.
6 Meanwhile, make plum and red wine sauce.
7 Serve sliced pork with sauce.
plum and red wine sauce Bring ingredients in small saucepan to the boil. Reduce heat; simmer, uncovered, about 10 minutes or until sauce thickens slightly.

preparation time 30 minutes
cooking time 1 hour 30 minutes serves 8
nutritional count per serving
30g total fat (8.6g saturated fat); 2934kJ (702 cal);
47.9g carbohydrate; 57.9g protein; 2.1g fibre

pork rack with roasted pears and parsnips

1kg rack of pork (6 cutlets), rind on
2 teaspoons olive oil
1 tablespoon sea salt flakes
2 small red onions (200g), quartered
2 medium parsnips (500g), quartered
3 small firm pears (540g), cored, quartered
4 cloves garlic, unpeeled
¼ cup (55g) firmly packed brown sugar
2 tablespoons olive oil, extra

1 Preheat oven to 220°C/200°C fan-forced.
2 Rub pork rind with oil then salt. Stand pork on wire rack in medium baking dish.
3 Combine remaining ingredients on oven tray.
4 Roast pork and pear mixture 25 minutes or until pork rind blisters; reduce oven to 180°C/160°C fan-forced, roast 25 minutes or until pork is cooked through.
5 Remove pork and pear mixture from oven, cover loosely with foil; stand pork 10 minutes before cutting. Serve pork with pear mixture.

preparation time 15 minutes
cooking time 55 minutes serves 6
nutritional count per serving
23g total fat (6.3g saturated fat); 1889kJ (452 cal);
29.3g carbohydrate; 29.6g protein; 4.7g fibre

pork rack with apple sage sauce

1kg rack of pork (6 cutlets), rind on
1 tablespoon olive oil
1 tablespoon sea salt flakes
1.25kg kipfler potatoes
750g pumpkin, chopped coarsely
apple sage sauce
3 large green apples (600g)
¼ cup (60ml) water
4 fresh sage leaves
1 teaspoon white sugar

1 Preheat oven to 220°C/200°C fan-forced.
2 Rub pork rind with half the oil then the salt. Stand pork in medium baking dish; roast, uncovered, about 35 minutes or until rind is blistered.
3 Place vegetables in oven tray with pork, drizzle with remaining oil. Reduce oven to 180°C/160°C fan-forced; roast pork and vegetables, uncovered, about 40 minutes or until pork is cooked through. Remove pork from dish; cover with foil to keep warm.
4 Meanwhile, make apple sage sauce.
5 Increase oven to 220°C/200°C fan-forced; roast vegetables for further 15 minutes. Serve pork with vegetables and apple sage sauce.
apple sage sauce Peel and core apples; slice thickly. Place apple, the water and sage in medium saucepan; simmer, uncovered, about 10 minutes or until apple is soft. Remove from heat, stir in sugar.

preparation time 20 minutes
cooking time 55 minutes serves 6
nutritional count per serving
19.5g total fat (6.7g saturated fat); 1914kJ (458 cal);
41.6g carbohydrate; 25.8g protein; 6.6g fibre
tip Kipfler are small finger-shaped potatoes. You can use quartered desiree or pontiac potatoes if you like.

grills & barbecues

plum sauce pork spare ribs with pear and chilli salad

2kg american-style pork ribs
1 cup (250ml) plum sauce
5cm piece fresh ginger (25g), grated
⅓ cup (80ml) oyster sauce
2 star anise
1 teaspoon dried chilli flakes
pear and chilli salad
2 medium pears (460g), sliced thinly
2 fresh long red chillies, sliced thinly
2 green onions, sliced thinly
2 cups coarsely chopped fresh mint
2cm piece fresh ginger (10g), grated
2 tablespoons lime juice

1 Combine pork with remaining ingredients in large shallow baking dish. Cover; refrigerate 3 hours or overnight, turning pork occasionally.
2 Preheat barbecue.
3 Drain pork; reserve marinade. Cook pork on heated oiled grill plate 20 minutes or until cooked through, turning and brushing frequently with reserved marinade.
4 Meanwhile, make pear and chilli salad.
5 Boil remaining marinade, uncovered, in small saucepan about 5 minutes or until thickened slightly.
6 Slice slabs into portions; serve with hot marinade and salad.
pear and chilli salad Place ingredients in medium bowl; toss gently to combine.

preparation time 25 minutes (plus refrigeration time)
cooking time 20 minutes **serves** 4
nutritional count per serving
18.1g total fat (6.6g saturated fat); 2847kJ (681 cal);
56.3g carbohydrate; 69.6g protein; 5.2g fibre

roasted peppered pork

1 tablespoon coarse cooking salt
1 tablespoon dried green peppercorns,
    crushed
1 tablespoon dried pink peppercorns,
    crushed
1 tablespoon white peppercorns, crushed
1 tablespoon black peppercorns, crushed
1kg boneless rolled shoulder of pork,
    rind on
cooking-oil spray

1   Preheat barbecue.
2   Combine salt and peppercorns in small bowl.
3   Score rind of pork, spray pork with oil.
Rub pepper mixture over pork.
4   Cook pork in disposable aluminium
baking dish, covered, using indirect heat,
about 1½ hours or until cooked.
5   Cover pork loosely with foil; stand
10 minutes, slice thickly.

preparation time 10 minutes
cooking time 1 hour 30 minutes serves 6
nutritional count per serving
19.2g total fat (7.3g saturated fat); 1371kJ (328 cal);
0g carbohydrate; 39g protein; 0g fibre

barbecue feast with warm potato salad

700g kipfler potatoes, halved lengthways
1 tablespoon olive oil
2 cloves garlic, crushed
2 teaspoons caraway seeds
½ small cabbage (600g), shredded coarsely
4 pork loin steaks (medallions) (400g)
4 thick pork sausages (480g)
4 thin rindless bacon rashers (120g)
⅓ cup (80ml) olive oil, extra
¼ cup (60ml) white wine vinegar
2 teaspoons dijon mustard

1   Preheat oven to 220°C/200°C fan-forced.
2   Combine potato, oil, garlic and seeds in
large shallow baking dish. Roast, uncovered,
about 30 minutes or until potato is browned.
3   Remove potato mixture from oven; stir in
cabbage. Return to oven; cook, uncovered,
about 15 minutes or until cabbage wilts.
4   Meanwhile, preheat barbecue.
5   Cook steaks, sausages and bacon, in
batches, on heated oiled grill plate. Remove
from heat; cover to keep warm.
6   Combine extra oil, vinegar and mustard
in large bowl with potato mixture.
7   Serve barbecue feast with potato salad.

preparation time 25 minutes
cooking time 45 minutes serves 4
nutritional count per serving
61g total fat (17.9g saturated fat); 2724kJ (891 cal);
31.2g carbohydrate; 49.7g protein; 10.1g fibre

pork cutlets with fennel relish and crushed herbed potatoes

2 tablespoons cider vinegar
¼ cup (60ml) olive oil
1 tablespoon dijon mustard
2 teaspoons white sugar
4 x 200g pork loin cutlets

fennel relish
1 large unpeeled green apple (200g),
    chopped finely
1 small red onion (100g), chopped finely
1 medium fennel bulb (300g),
    trimmed, chopped finely

crushed herbed potatoes
1kg baby new potatoes, unpeeled
½ cup (120g) sour cream
40g butter, softened
2 tablespoons corasely chopped fresh dill
¼ cup coarsely chopped fresh
    flat-leaf parsley

1 Preheat barbecue.
2 Whisk vinegar, oil, mustard and sugar in medium bowl; transfer 2 tablespoons of dressing to large bowl. Reserve remaining dressing for fennel relish. Place pork in large bowl; turn to coat in dressing.
3 Meanwhile, make fennel relish and crushed herbed potatoes.
4 Cook drained pork on heated oiled grill plate until browned both sides and cooked through, brushing with dressing occasionally.
5 Serve pork with relish and crushed herbed potatoes.

fennel relish Combine ingredients in medium bowl with reserved dressing.
crushed herbed potatoes Boil, steam or microwave potatoes until tender; drain. Mash half the potatoes with sour cream and butter in large bowl until smooth; stir in dill and parsley. Roughly crush remaining potatoes until skins burst; stir into herbed mash.

preparation time 20 minutes
cooking time 20 minutes **serves** 4
nutritional count per serving
16g total fat (2.7g saturated fat); 1283kJ (307 cal);
9.4g carbohydrate; 30.2g protein; 2.4g fibre

teriyaki pork with pineapple

⅓ cup (80ml) mirin
¼ cup (60ml) japanese soy sauce
2 tablespoons cooking sake
2 teaspoons white sugar
5cm piece fresh ginger (25g), grated
2 cloves garlic, crushed
600g pork fillet
1 small pineapple (900g), sliced thinly
2 green onions, sliced thinly

1 Combine mirin, sauce, sake, sugar, ginger and garlic in large bowl; add pork, turn to coat in marinade. Cover; refrigerate 3 hours or overnight.

2 Preheat barbecue.

3 Drain pork; reserve marinade. Cook pork on heated oiled grill plate until browned and cooked as desired. Cover loosely with foil; stand 10 minutes.

4 Cook pineapple on grill plate 2 minutes or until soft.

5 Bring reserved marinade to the boil in small saucepan; cook about 5 minutes or until sauce reduces by half.

6 Serve sliced pork with pineapple and onion; drizzle with sauce.

preparation time 20 minutes (plus refrigeration time)
cooking time 20 minutes serves 4
nutritional count per serving
2.6g total fat (0.7g saturated fat); 1045kJ (250 cal);
13.3g carbohydrate; 36.2g protein; 3g fibre

sage roasted pork loin

10 fresh sage leaves
1kg boneless loin of pork, rind off
2 tablespoons sea salt flakes
2 tablespoons crushed dried
    green peppercorns
2 tablespoons coarsely chopped fresh sage
1 tablespoon olive oil

1 Preheat barbecue.

2 Lay sage leaves in the middle of pork loin; roll pork to enclose leaves. Tie pork at 10cm intervals with kitchen string.

3 Combine salt, peppercorns and chopped sage in small bowl.

4 Brush pork with oil; rub with salt mixture.

5 Place pork in disposable aluminium baking dish. Cook pork in covered barbecue, using indirect heat, about 1 hour or until cooked through.

6 Cover pork loosely with foil; stand for 10 minutes before slicing.

preparation time 15 minutes (plus standing time)
cooking time 1 hour serves 6
nutritional count per serving
5.7g total fat (1.3g saturated fat); 861kJ (206 cal);
0.7g carbohydrate; 37.7g protein; 0g fibre

pork silverside roast with maple-roasted vegies

1 tablespoon olive oil
1.2kg pork silverside roast
¼ teaspoon ground cinnamon
¼ teaspoon ground ginger
1 large kumara (500g), peeled,
    chopped coarsely
600g piece pumpkin, peeled,
    chopped coarsely
1 cup (250ml) pure maple syrup
⅔ cup (160ml) barbecue sauce

1 Preheat barbecue.
2 Brush pork with oil; place on heated grill plate, cook, turning, until browned all over. Remove from barbecue; place in disposable aluminium baking dish.
3 Combine cinnamon, ginger, vegetables, syrup and sauce in large bowl. Place vegetable mixture around pork in baking dish; brush pork with a little of the sauce.
4 Cook pork and vegetables, covered, using indirect heat, about 1¼ hours. Stand pork, covered loosely with foil, for 10 minutes before slicing thickly.
5 Serve with maple-roasted vegetables.

preparation time 10 minutes (plus standing time)
cooking time 1 hour 35 minutes serves 4
nutritional count per serving
10.2g total fat (2.5g saturated fat); 3277kJ (784 cal);
96.4g carbohydrate; 72.7g protein; 3.8g fibre

hoisin pork kebabs

750g pork fillet, sliced
½ cup (125ml) hoisin sauce
2 tablespoons plum sauce
2 cloves garlic, crushed

1 Combine pork, sauces and garlic in medium bowl. Cover, refrigerate 3 hours or overnight.
2 Preheat barbecue.
3 Thread pork onto 12 skewers. Cook kebabs on heated oiled grill plate until browned and cooked through.

preparation time 10 minutes (plus marinating time)
cooking time 10 minutes serves 4
nutritional count per serving
8.2g total fat (2g saturated fat); 1630kJ (390 cal);
33.3g carbohydrate; 42.8g protein; 4.4g fibre

indian pork kebabs with mango chutney

1kg pork fillet
¼ cup (75g) madras curry paste
¾ cup (210g) yogurt
2 tablespoons lemon juice
2 large red capsicums (700g)
2 large brown onions (400g)
1 cup (320g) mango chutney

1 Cut pork into 2cm cubes. Whisk paste, yogurt and juice in medium bowl until smooth; add pork. Cover; refrigerate 3 hours or overnight.
2 Preheat barbecue.
3 Cut capsicums into 4cm pieces; cut onions into wedges. Thread pork, capsicum and onion onto 12 skewers.
4 Cook kebabs on heated oiled grill plate, uncovered, until browned and cooked through.
5 Serve kebabs with mango chutney.

preparation time 45 minutes (plus marinating time)
cooking time 15 minutes serves 6
nutritional count per serving
4.9g total fat (1.2g saturated fat); 1258kJ (301 cal);
18.4g carbohydrate; 43.1g protein; 3.8g fibre

teriyaki pork with wasabi dressing

750g pork fillet
¼ cup (60ml) teriyaki marinade
50g snow pea sprouts
100g mesclun
50g watercress, trimmed
1 medium red capsicum (200g),
    sliced thinly
250g yellow teardrop tomatoes, halved
wasabi dressing
1½ teaspoons wasabi powder
¼ cup (60ml) cider vinegar
⅓ cup (80ml) vegetable oil
1 tablespoon japanese soy sauce

1 Preheat barbecue.
2 Brush pork with teriyaki marinade. Cook pork, in batches, uncovered, on heated oiled grill plate, brushing frequently with marinade, until browned and cooked through; cover to keep warm.
3 Meanwhile, make wasabi dressing.
4 Place sprouts, mesclun, watercress, capsicum and tomato in large bowl with dressing; toss gently to combine.
5 Slice pork; serve with salad.
wasabi dressing Blend wasabi powder with vinegar in small jug; whisk in remaining ingredients.

preparation time 15 minutes
cooking time 10 minutes serves 4
nutritional count per serving
22g total fat (3.4g saturated fat); 1747kJ (418 cal);
7.2g carbohydrate; 46.3g protein; 3.1g fibre

spiced pork kebabs with honey glaze

500g pork fillet
2 cloves garlic, crushed
2 teaspoons cumin seeds
½ teaspoon ground coriander
¼ teaspoon sweet paprika
1 tablespoon olive oil
honey glaze
½ cup (125ml) orange juice
2 tablespoons honey
2 tablespoons barbecue sauce
1 teaspoon dijon mustard

1 Preheat barbecue.
2 Cut pork into 3cm cubes. Combine pork with garlic, cumin, coriander, paprika and oil in medium bowl. Thread pork onto eight skewers.
3 Cook kebabs on heated oiled grill plate until browned and cooked through.
4 Meanwhile, make honey glaze.
5 Serve kebabs with glaze.
honey glaze Stir ingredients in small saucepan over heat until boiling. Reduce heat; simmer 5 minutes or until thickened.

preparation time 15 minutes
cooking time 15 minutes makes 8
nutritional count per kebab
3.3g total fat (0.6g saturated fat); 531kJ (127 cal);
9.7g carbohydrate; 14.3g protein; 0.2g fibre

mexican pork cutlets with avocado salsa

2 tablespoons taco seasoning mix
¼ cup (60ml) olive oil
4 x 200g pork loin cutlets
3 small tomatoes (270g), seeded,
    chopped finely
1 small avocado (200g), chopped finely
1 lebanese cucumber (130g), seeded,
    chopped finely
1 tablespoon lime juice

1 Preheat barbecue.
2 Combine seasoning, 2 tablespoons of
the oil and pork in large bowl. Cook pork
on heated oiled grill plate.
3 Meanwhile, combine remaining oil in
medium bowl with tomato, avocado,
cucumber and juice.
4 Serve pork with salsa.

preparation time 10 minutes
cooking time 10 minutes serves 4
nutritional count per serving
23.8g total fat (4.4g saturated fat); 1421kJ (340 cal);
1.2g carbohydrate; 30.2g protein; 1.2g fibre

grilled pork loin chops with apple and onion plum sauce

2 medium apples (300g)
1 tablespoon olive oil
1 medium red onion (170g),
    cut into thin wedges
4 x 280g pork loin chops
½ cup (125ml) plum sauce
¼ cup (60ml) lemon juice
⅓ cup (80ml) chicken stock

1 Preheat barbecue.
2 Cut each unpeeled, uncored apple
horizontally into four slices. Heat oil in
grill pan; cook apple and onion, turning,
until softened.
3 Meanwhile, cook pork on heated oiled
grill plate.
4 Stir sauce, juice and stock into apple
mixture; simmer 1 minute.
5 Serve pork with sauce.

preparation time 10 minutes
cooking time 20 minutes serves 4
nutritional count per serving
8.7g total fat (1.9g saturated fat); 1718kJ (411 cal);
31.8g carbohydrate; 49.7g protein; 1.8g fibre

spicy pork chops with pumpkin chips

Piri piri, an Afro-Portuguese hot sauce, is made from a tiny red chilli of the same name, ground with ginger, garlic, oil and various herbs. It can be used in a marinade or as an ingredient, but most often applied as a glaze, brushed constantly over meat or poultry as it's being grilled.

3 fresh long green chillies,
    chopped coarsely
3 green onions, chopped coarsely
2 cloves garlic, crushed
1 teaspoon ground allspice
1 teaspoon dried thyme
1 teaspoon white sugar
1 tablespoon light soy sauce
1 tablespoon lime juice
4 x 280g pork loin chops
1kg piece pumpkin, trimmed
2 tablespoons vegetable oil
piri piri dipping sauce
⅓ cup (100g) mayonnaise
2 tablespoons piri piri sauce

1 Combine chilli, onion, garlic, allspice, thyme, sugar, sauce, juice and pork in medium bowl.
2 Combine ingredients for piri piri dipping sauce in small bowl.
3 Preheat barbecue.
4 Cut pumpkin into 7cm chips; boil, steam or microwave until tender. Drain; combine chips with oil in medium bowl. Cook chips on heated oiled grill plate until browned.
5 Meanwhile, cook pork on heated oiled grill plate.
6 Serve pork with chips and dipping sauce.

preparation time 15 minutes
cooking time 25 minutes serves 4
nutritional count per serving
21.4g total fat (3.8g saturated fat); 1965kJ (470 cal);
21.6g carbohydrate; 46g protein; 3.6g fibre

grilled pork medallions with capsicum cream sauce

1 medium red capsicum (200g)
1 medium tomato (150g), halved, seeded
2 teaspoons olive oil
1 clove garlic, crushed
1 small brown onion (80g), chopped finely
½ trimmed celery stalk (50g), chopped finely
2 tablespoons water
1 teaspoon finely chopped fresh rosemary
4 x 150g pork loin medallions, thick cut
½ cup (125ml) cream

1 Preheat barbecue.
2 Quarter capsicum; discard seeds and membranes. Roast capsicum and tomato on barbecue until capsicum skin blisters and blackens. Cover capsicum and tomato with foil for 5 minutes; peel away skins then slice capsicum thickly.
3 Heat oil in small frying pan; cook garlic, onion and celery until softened. Add capsicum, tomato and the water; cook, uncovered, 5 minutes. Remove from heat; stir in rosemary.
4 Meanwhile, cook pork on heated oiled grill plate. Cover to keep warm.
5 Blend or process capsicum mixture until smooth. Return to same pan, add cream; bring to the boil. Reduce heat; simmer, uncovered, 5 minutes.
6 Serve pork with sauce.

preparation time 15 minutes
cooking time 15 minutes **serves** 4
nutritional count per serving
18.4g total fat (10g saturated fat); 1384kJ (331 cal); 4.7g carbohydrate; 36g protein; 1.8g fibre

chinese barbecued pork

1kg pork scotch fillet
marinade
2 star anise, crushed
2 tablespoons light soy sauce
2 tablespoons brown sugar
1½ tablespoons honey
1½ tablespoons dry sherry
2 teaspoons hoisin sauce
2cm piece fresh ginger (10g), grated
1 clove garlic, crushed
2 green onions, chopped finely
few drops red food colouring

1 Cut pork into quarters lengthways.
2 Combine ingredients for marinade in large shallow dish; add pork, toss to combine. Cover; refrigerate 3 hours or overnight.
3 Preheat barbecue.
4 Drain pork; reserve marinade. Cook pork on heated oiled barbecue, uncovered, until browned and cooked through, brushing with reserved marinade during cooking.

preparation time 15 minutes (plus marinating time)
cooking time 15 minutes **serves** 6
nutritional count per serving
13.5g total fat (4.5g saturated fat); 1321kJ (316 cal); 11.3g carbohydrate; 35.9g protein; 0.4g fibre

barbecued pork spare ribs with red cabbage coleslaw

2kg american-style pork ribs

barbecue sauce

1 cup (250ml) tomato sauce
¾ cup (180ml) cider vinegar
2 tablespoons olive oil
¼ cup (60ml) worcestershire sauce
⅓ cup (75g) firmly packed brown sugar
2 tablespoons american mustard
1 teaspoon cracked black pepper
2 fresh small red thai chillies,
   chopped finely
2 cloves garlic, crushed
2 tablespoons lemon juice

red cabbage coleslaw

½ cup (120g) sour cream
¼ cup (60ml) lemon juice
2 tablespoons water
½ small red cabbage (600g), shredded finely
3 green onions, sliced thinly

1 Make barbecue sauce.
2 Place ribs in large shallow baking dish; pour barbecue sauce over ribs. Cover; refrigerate 3 hours or overnight, turning ribs occasionally.
3 Make red cabbage coleslaw.
4 Preheat barbecue.
5 Drain ribs; reserve sauce. Cook ribs on heated oiled grill plate, brushing occasionally with reserved sauce, about 15 minutes or until cooked. Turn ribs halfway through cooking time.
6 Bring remaining sauce to the boil in small saucepan; boil about 4 minutes or until sauce thickens slightly.
7 Cut ribs into serving-sized pieces; serve with hot barbecue sauce and coleslaw.

barbecue sauce Bring ingredients in medium saucepan to the boil. Cool 10 minutes.

red cabbage coleslaw Place sour cream, juice and the water in screw-top jar; shake well. Place cabbage and onion in large bowl with dressing; toss gently to combine.

preparation time 15 minutes (plus refrigeration time)
cooking time 25 minutes serves 4
nutritional count per serving
39.9g total fat (15.2g saturated fat); 3210kJ (768 cal); 44.4g carbohydrate; 53.6g protein; 8g fibre

pork and mandarin salad

2 star anise, crushed
2 tablespoons dark soy sauce
1 tablespoon hoisin sauce
2 tablespoons brown sugar
1 tablespoon honey
1 tablespoon dry sherry
5cm piece fresh ginger (25g), grated
1 clove garlic, crushed
few drops red food colouring
1kg pork scotch fillet
565g can lychees in syrup, drained
2 medium mandarins (400g), segmented
4 green onions, sliced thinly
½ cup (75g) roasted, unsalted cashews
2½ cups (200g) bean sprouts

1 Combine star anise, sauces, sugar, honey, sherry, ginger, garlic and colouring in medium bowl. Add pork, turn to coat in marinade. Cover; refrigerate 3 hours or overnight.
2 Preheat barbecue.
3 Drain pork; discard marinade.
4 Place pork in disposable aluminium baking dish; cook, covered, using indirect heat, about 1 hour or until cooked through. Cover loosely with foil, stand 5 minutes.
5 Combine remaining ingredients for salad on serving plate; top with sliced pork.

preparation time 25 minutes (plus marinating time)
cooking time 1 hour (plus standing time) serves 6
nutritional count per serving
19.9g total fat (5.6g saturated fat); 1877kJ (449 cal); 24.6g carbohydrate; 39.9g protein; 4g fibre

sausages with tomato relish

1 tablespoon olive oil
1 clove garlic, crushed
1 medium brown onion (150g), chopped
2 large tomatoes (500g), chopped coarsely
1 tablespoon balsamic vinegar
1 teaspoon brown sugar
1 tablespoon torn fresh basil leaves
8 thin pork sausages

1 Heat oil in small saucepan; cook garlic and onion, stirring, until browned lightly. Add tomato, vinegar and sugar; simmer, uncovered, stirring occasionally, about 20 minutes or until mixture is reduced by half. Just before serving, add basil.
2 Preheat barbecue.
3 Cook sausages on heated oiled grill plate. Serve sausages with warm tomato relish.

preparation time 10 minutes
cooking time 30 minutes serves 4
nutritional count per serving
30.5g total fat (11.1g saturated fat); 1576kJ (377 cal); 9g carbohydrate; 15.8g protein; 3.6g fibre

pan-fries

favourite spaghetti bolognaise

You can add a little spicy sausage, bacon or chilli to this recipe for a delicious change.

2 tablespoons olive oil
500g pork mince
1 medium brown onion (150g), chopped finely
2 cloves garlic, chopped finely
2 teaspoons dried italian herbs
2 tablespoons tomato paste
400g can diced tomatoes
1 cup (250ml) chicken stock
½ cup (125ml) dry red wine
½ cup (60g) seeded green olives, chopped coarsely
½ cup coarsely chopped fresh flat-leaf parsley
375g spaghetti

1 Heat 1 tablespoon of the oil in medium frying pan; cook pork, stirring, until browned. Remove from pan.
2 Heat remaining oil in same pan; cook onion and garlic, stirring, until onion softens.
3 Return pork to pan with herbs, paste, undrained tomatoes, stock and wine. Cook, stirring, until mixture boils. Reduce heat; simmer, uncovered, 30 minutes, stirring occasionally.
4 Meanwhile, cook pasta, uncovered, in large saucepan of boiling water until just tender; drain.
5 Stir olives and parsley into mince mixture. Serve spaghetti, topped with bolognaise and sprinkled with grated parmesan cheese, if desired.

preparation time 10 minutes
cooking time 45 minutes serves 4
nutritional count per serving
14g total fat (2.6g saturated fat); 2587kJ (619 cal); 71.5g carbohydrate; 46.6g protein; 6.3g fibre

warm pork and mandarin salad with honey dressing

600g pork fillet
2 medium mandarins (400g), peeled
2 tablespoons olive oil
1 tablespoon honey
1 fresh long red chilli, chopped finely
2 medium radicchio (400g), trimmed
1 cup (50g) snow pea sprouts
¾ cup (115g) roasted unsalted cashews

1 Cook pork, uncovered, in heated oiled large frying pan until cooked as desired. Cover; stand 5 minutes then slice thickly.
2 Meanwhile, segment mandarins into large bowl. Stir in combined oil, honey and chilli. Add pork, radicchio, sprouts and nuts; toss gently to combine.
3 Serve salad warm.

preparation time 10 minutes
cooking time 10 minutes serves 4
nutritional count per serving
26.2g total fat (4.6g saturated fat); 2077kJ (497 cal);
20.7g carbohydrate; 42.1g protein; 5.9g fibre

pork fillet with cranberry crumble and red wine sauce

1 tablespoon olive oil
1 medium brown onion (150g), chopped finely
1 clove garlic, crushed
2 tablespoons dried cranberries
60g baby spinach leaves
½ cup (35g) stale breadcrumbs
¼ cup (40g) roasted pine nuts
600g pork fillet
½ cup (125ml) dry red wine
¾ cup (180ml) chicken stock
2 tablespoons redcurrant jelly

1 Heat oil in large frying pan; cook onion and garlic, stirring, until onion softens. Add cranberries and spinach; cook, stirring, until spinach wilts. Combine cranberry mixture with breadcrumbs and nuts in medium bowl. Cover to keep warm.
2 Cook pork, uncovered, in same pan until cooked as desired. Cover; stand 5 minutes then slice thickly.
3 Meanwhile, bring wine to the boil in small saucepan. Reduce heat; simmer, uncovered, until reduced by half. Add stock and jelly; cook, uncovered, about 10 minutes, stirring occasionally, or until sauce thickens.
4 Serve pork with cranberry crumble, drizzled with sauce.

preparation time 20 minutes
cooking time 20 minutes serves 4
nutritional count per serving
14.6g total fat (2g saturated fat); 1672kJ (400 cal);
22.4g carbohydrate; 38.1g protein; 2.4g fibre

pork cutlets with stuffed apple and peppercorn cider sauce

40g butter
1 small brown onion (80g), chopped finely
1 clove garlic, crushed
1 rindless bacon rasher (65g),
    chopped finely
¼ cup (15g) stale breadcrumbs
2 seeded prunes (20g), chopped finely
2 tablespoons finely chopped fresh chives
2 large unpeeled apples (400g)
10g butter, extra
4 x 200g pork loin cutlets
½ cup (125ml) sparkling apple cider
2 teaspoons drained green peppercorns,
    crushed
300ml cream

1 Preheat oven to 180°C/160°C fan-forced.
2 Melt butter in large frying pan; cook onion, garlic and bacon, stirring, until onion softens. Stir in breadcrumbs, prunes and half of the chives.
3 Core apples; pierce apples in several places with fork. Press breadcrumb mixture into apple centres; place in small baking dish. Melt extra butter; brush all over apples. Cook, uncovered, about 40 minutes.
4 Meanwhile, cook pork in same cleaned pan. Cover loosely with foil.
5 Remove apples from dish; cover to keep warm. Add cider and peppercorns to dish; cook, stirring, 1 minute. Add cream; bring to the boil. Reduce heat; simmer, uncovered, until sauce thickens slightly. Stir in remaining chives. Halve apples; serve with pork, drizzle with sauce.

preparation time 20 minutes
cooking time 1 hour serves 4
nutritional count per serving
46.7g total fat (29.5g saturated fat); 2713kJ (649 cal); 21.2g carbohydrate; 35.8g protein; 2.6g fibre

cashew, lemon and thyme crumbed pork schnitzels

4 x 150g pork leg schnitzels
1 cup (150g) roasted unsalted cashews
½ cup (35g) stale breadcrumbs
2 teaspoons finely grated lemon rind
2 teaspoons finely chopped fresh thyme
1 egg
vegetable oil, for shallow-frying
1 medium lemon (140g), cut into wedges

1 Using meat mallet, gently pound pork, one piece at a time, between sheets of plastic wrap, until about 5mm in thickness.
2 Blend or process nuts until coarsely chopped; combine in shallow medium bowl with breadcrumbs, rind and thyme. Whisk egg lightly in another shallow medium bowl. Dip pork in egg then coat in cashew mixture.
3 Heat oil in large frying pan; cook pork, in batches. Drain on absorbent paper. Serve pork with lemon.

preparation time 20 minutes
cooking time 15 minutes serves 4
nutritional count per serving
34.7g total fat (6g saturated); 2266kJ (542 cal); 13g carbohydrate; 43.6g protein; 3.3g fibre

chilli pork burgers

700g pork mince
1 small red onion (100g), chopped finely
⅓ cup coarsely chopped fresh coriander
1 egg
1 fresh long red chilli, chopped finely
¼ cup (15g) stale breadcrumbs
4 hamburger buns (360g)
⅓ cup (100g) mayonnaise
50g mizuna
⅓ cup (25g) fried shallots
sweet chilli salsa
1 medium red capsicum (200g),
    sliced thinly
1 large red onion (300g), sliced thinly
½ cup (125ml) sweet chilli sauce

1 Combine pork, onion, coriander, egg, chilli and breadcrumbs in large bowl; shape mixture into four patties.
2 Cook patties in heated oiled large frying pan.
3 Meanwhile, make sweet chilli salsa.
4 Split buns in half; toast cut sides. Spread buns with mayonnaise, fill with mizuna, patties, salsa and shallots.
sweet chilli salsa Cook capsicum and onion in heated oiled medium frying pan until onion softens. Add sauce; cook, stirring gently, 2 minutes or until mixture caramelises.

preparation time 15 minutes
cooking time 20 minutes serves 4
nutritional count per serving
18.2g total fat (3.3g saturated fat); 2809kJ (672 cal);
68.6g carbohydrate; 53.9g protein; 7.2g fibre

pork schnitzels with lemon and parsley crumb

2 cups (140g) stale breadcrumbs
2 tablespoons finely grated lemon rind
2 tablespoons finely chopped fresh
    flat-leaf parsley
2 cloves garlic, crushed
4 x 150g pork leg schnitzel
⅓ cup (50g) plain flour
1 egg
2 tablespoons milk
vegetable oil, for shallow-frying

1 Combine breadcrumbs, rind, parsley and garlic in medium bowl.
2 Toss pork in flour, shake away excess.
3 Dip pork in combined egg and milk, then in breadcrumb mixture.
4 Heat oil in large frying pan; cook pork over medium heat until browned both sides and cooked through.

preparation time 10 minutes
cooking time 20 minutes serves 4
nutritional count per serving
17.2g total fat (3.3g saturated fat); 1965kJ (470 cal);
33.8g carbohydrate; 43.2g protein; 2.6g fibre

beetroot and lentil salad with pork sausages

1½ cups (350g) brown lentils
2 sprigs fresh thyme
850g small beetroots, trimmed
1 tablespoon olive oil
1 large brown onion (200g), chopped finely
2 teaspoons yellow mustard seeds
2 teaspoons ground cumin
1 teaspoon ground coriander
½ cup (125ml) chicken stock
150g baby spinach leaves
8 thick pork sausages (960g)
thyme dressing
1 teaspoon fresh thyme leaves
1 clove garlic, crushed
½ cup (125ml) red wine vinegar
¼ cup (60ml) olive oil

1 Place ingredients for thyme dressing in screw-top jar; shake well.
2 Cook lentils and thyme, uncovered, in large saucepan of boiling water until lentils are just tender; drain, discard thyme. Combine lentils in large bowl with half of the dressing.
3 Meanwhile, discard any leaves and all but 2cm of the stalk from each beetroot. Boil, steam or microwave unpeeled beetroots until just tender; drain. When cool enough to handle, peel then quarter each beetroot; place in bowl with lentils.
4 Heat oil in large frying pan; cook onion, seeds and spices, stirring, until onion softens. Add stock; bring to the boil. Remove from heat; stir in spinach.
5 Combine spinach mixture with remaining dressing in medium bowl with beetroot and lentil mixture.
6 Cook sausages in same cleaned pan.
7 Serve sliced sausages with salad.

preparation time 25 minutes
cooking time 50 minutes serves 4
nutritional count per serving
73.7g total fat (24.5g saturated fat); 4623kJ (1106 cal); 58.7g carbohydrate; 55.5g protein; 22.6g fibre

tonkatsu-don

Koshihikari rice is a small, round-grain white rice. If unavailable, substitute with a short-grain rice such as arborio. Prepared tonkatsu sauce is sold in most supermarkets and Asian food stores if you don't wish to make your own.

3 cups (750ml) water
1½ cups (300g) koshihikari rice
4 x 150g pork leg steaks
¼ cup (35g) plain flour
2 eggs
2 teaspoons water, extra
2 cups (100g) japanese breadcrumbs
1 tablespoon peanut oil
2 cloves garlic, sliced thinly
½ small wombok (350g), shredded finely
1 fresh small red thai chilli, chopped finely
1 tablespoon mirin
1 tablespoon japanese soy sauce
vegetable oil, for shallow-frying
2 green onions, sliced thinly
tonkatsu sauce
⅓ cup (80ml) tomato sauce
2 tablespoons japanese worcestershire sauce
2 tablespoons cooking sake
1 teaspoon japanese soy sauce
1 teaspoon japanese mustard

1 Make tonkatsu sauce.
2 Bring the water and rice in medium saucepan to the boil. Reduce heat; cook, covered tightly, over very low heat, about 15 minutes or until water is absorbed. Remove from heat; stand, covered, 10 minutes.
3 Meanwhile, pound pork gently with meat mallet; coat in flour, shake off excess. Dip pork in combined eggs and extra water then coat in breadcrumbs.
4 Heat peanut oil in large frying pan; cook garlic, stirring, until fragrant. Add wombok and chilli; cook, stirring, 1 minute. Transfer wombok mixture to large bowl, sprinkle with mirin and sauce. Cover to keep warm.
5 Heat vegetable oil in same cleaned pan; shallow-fry pork, in batches, about 5 minutes or until golden brown. Drain on absorbent paper. Cut pork diagonally into 2cm slices.
6 Divide rice among serving bowls; top with pork, wombok mixture then onion and drizzle with tonkatsu sauce.
tonkatsu sauce Place ingredients in small saucepan; bring to the boil. Remove from heat; cool.

preparation time 25 minutes
cooking time 30 minutes serves 4
nutritional count per serving
17.8g total fat (3.3g saturated fat); 3160kJ (756 cal); 91.1g carbohydrate; 51.2g protein; 4g fibre
tip Japanese breadcrumbs, also known as panko, are available from Asian grocers and some supermarkets. If you can't find the Japanese variety, use stale breadcrumbs, instead.

stir-fries

sticky pork with vegies

1 tablespoon honey
2 tablespoons light soy sauce
2 tablespoons brown sugar
1 teaspoon five-spice powder
1 teaspoon hot chilli powder
3 cloves garlic, crushed
1 teaspoon sesame oil
750g pork scotch fillet, cut into 3cm cubes
2 tablespoons peanut oil
½ cup (70g) raw peanuts, chopped coarsely
1 medium carrot (120g), cut into matchsticks
150g snow peas, trimmed,
    sliced thinly lengthways
2 tablespoons orange juice
3 kaffir lime leaves, shredded
4 green onions, sliced thinly

1 Combine honey, sauce, sugar, five-spice, chilli, garlic and sesame oil in large bowl; add pork, turn to coat in marinade. Cover; refrigerate 3 hours or overnight.
2 Heat half the peanut oil in wok; stir-fry nuts until browned. Drain.
3 Heat remaining peanut oil in wok. Add pork; stir-fry, in batches, until browned. Return pork to wok with carrot; stir-fry until pork is cooked.
4 Add snow peas, juice and lime leaves; stir-fry until snow peas are tender. Remove from heat; toss in onion and nuts.

preparation time 15 minutes (plus refrigeration time)
cooking time 25 minutes serves 4
nutritional count per serving
33.7g total fat (8.1g saturated fat); 2366kJ (566 cal);
18.5g carbohydrate; 46.4g protein; 3.8g fibre

chilli pork with oyster sauce

1 tablespoon peanut oil
450g pork fillet, sliced thinly
1 clove garlic, crushed
1 medium white onion (150g), sliced thinly
1 large red capsicum (350g), sliced thinly
1 small green zucchini (90g), sliced thinly
1 small yellow zucchini (90g), sliced thinly
¼ cup (60ml) oyster sauce
1 tablespoon sweet chilli sauce
1 tablespoon coarsely chopped
    fresh coriander

1 Heat oil in wok; stir-fry pork, in batches, until browned.
2 Stir-fry garlic and onion. Add capsicum and zucchini; stir-fry.
3 Return pork to wok. Add sauces; stir-fry until hot. Serve sprinkled with coriander.

preparation time 15 minutes
cooking time 10 minutes serves 4
nutritional count per serving
7g total fat (1.4g saturated fat); 941kJ (225 cal);
10.5g carbohydrate; 28.5g protein; 2.4g fibre

jungle pork stir-fry

This recipe is a variation of Thai jungle pork curry – rated one of the hottest!

1 tablespoon peanut oil
1kg pork fillet, sliced thinly
1 medium brown onion (150g),
    sliced thinly
2 fresh small red thai chillies,
    sliced thinly
1 tablespoon finely chopped lemon grass
1 tablespoon drained, green peppercorns,
    chopped coarsely
1 tablespoon grated palm sugar
1 tablespoon finely grated fresh galangal
4 fresh kaffir lime leaves, shredded finely
2 tablespoons green curry paste
100g thai eggplants, halved
1 cup (250ml) coconut cream
¼ cup loosely packed fresh thai basil leaves

1 Heat oil in wok; stir-fry pork and onion, in batches, until pork is browned all over.
2 Add chilli, lemon grass, peppercorns, sugar, galangal, lime leaves and paste to wok; stir-fry until fragrant.
3 Return pork mixture to wok with eggplant and coconut cream; stir-fry until eggplant is just tender. Stir in basil.

preparation time 15 minutes
cooking time 15 minutes serves 4
nutritional count per serving
25.2g total fat (13.8g saturated fat); 2136kJ (511 cal);
10g carbohydrate; 59.2g protein; 3.7g fibre
tip Galangal is a dried root with a piquant peppery flavour. You can substitute fresh ginger for the galangal, if unavailable.

pork with sweet and sour peaches

2 tablespoons cornflour
800g pork fillet, sliced thinly
2 tablespoons peanut oil
1 medium red onion (170g),
    chopped coarsely
1 medium red capsicum (200g),
    cut into thin strips
1 medium yellow capsicum (200g),
    cut into thin strips
⅓ cup (80ml) water
2 cloves garlic, crushed
2 tablespoons white sugar
2 tablespoons white wine vinegar
2 tablespoons tomato sauce
2 tablespoons light soy sauce
2 large peaches (440g), cut into wedges
⅓ cup coarsely chopped fresh coriander

1 Rub cornflour into pork in medium bowl.
2 Heat half the oil in wok; stir-fry pork, in batches, until browned.
3 Heat remaining oil in wok; stir-fry onion and capsicums until tender.
4 Return pork to wok with the water, garlic, sugar, vinegar and sauces; stir-fry until pork is cooked. Add peach; stir-fry until hot. Serve sprinkled with coriander.

....

preparation time 20 minutes
cooking time 10 minutes **serves** 4
nutritional count per serving
12.6g total fat (2.7g saturated fat); 1772kJ (424 cal);
26.9g carbohydrate; 48.7g protein; 3g fibre
tip If peaches are not in season, use a 410g can of peaches in natural juice. Drain the peaches well and add them to the stir-fry after the pork is cooked. Stir-fry over high heat until peaches are hot.

curried fried rice with pork and prawns

800g pork leg steaks, sliced thinly
1 tablespoon white sugar
2 tablespoons light soy sauce
125g uncooked small prawns
2 tablespoons peanut oil
2 eggs, beaten lightly
1 teaspoon curry powder
2 cloves garlic, crushed
2 cups cold cooked white long-grain rice
4 green onions, sliced thinly
2 cups (240g) frozen peas and corn

1 Combine pork in medium bowl with sugar and half the sauce. Shell and devein prawns, leaving tails intact.

2 Heat 1 teaspoon of the oil in wok. Pour egg into wok; cook over medium heat, tilting wok, until egg is almost set. Remove omelette from wok; roll tightly, slice thinly.

3 Heat 2 teaspoons of the remaining oil in wok; stir-fry pork, in batches, until cooked.

4 Heat 1 teaspoon of remaining oil in wok; stir-fry prawns until just changed in colour. Remove from wok.

5 Heat remaining oil in wok; cook curry powder and garlic, stirring, until fragrant. Add rice, onion, pea and corn mixture and remaining sauce; stir-fry until vegetables are just tender.

6 Return pork, prawns and half of the omelette to wok; stir-fry until hot. Sprinkle fried rice with remaining omelette.

preparation time 20 minutes
cooking time 25 minutes serves 4
nutritional count per serving
15.1g total fat (3.3g saturated fat); 2228kJ (533 cal);
38g carbohydrate; 58.3g protein; 4.9g fibre

san choy bau

2 teaspoons sesame oil
1 small brown onion (80g), chopped finely
2 cloves garlic, crushed
2cm piece fresh ginger (10g), grated
500g pork mince
2 tablespoons water
100g shiitake mushrooms, chopped finely
2 tablespoons light soy sauce
2 tablespoons oyster sauce
1 tablespoon lime juice
2 cups (160g) bean sprouts
4 green onions, sliced thinly
¼ cup coarsely chopped fresh coriander
12 large butter lettuce leaves

1 Heat oil in wok; stir-fry brown onion, garlic and ginger until onion softens. Add pork; stir-fry until changed in colour.

2 Add the water, mushrooms, sauces and juice; stir-fry until mushrooms are tender. Remove from heat. Add sprouts, green onion and coriander; toss to combine.

3 Spoon san choy bau into lettuce leaves.

preparation time 15 minutes
cooking time 15 minutes serves 4
nutritional count per serving
5.5g total fat (1.3g saturated fat); 915kJ (219 cal);
6.5g carbohydrate; 33.4g protein; 4.1g fibre

stir-fried pork with buk choy and rice noodles

¼ cup (60ml) oyster sauce
2 tablespoons light soy sauce
2 tablespoons sweet sherry
1 tablespoon brown sugar
1 clove garlic, crushed
1 star anise, crushed
pinch five-spice powder
400g fresh rice noodles
2 teaspoons sesame oil
600g pork fillet, sliced thinly
700g baby buk choy, chopped coarsely

1 Combine sauces, sherry, sugar, garlic, star anise and five-spice in small jug.
2 Place noodles in large heatproof bowl, cover with boiling water; separate noodles with fork, drain.
3 Heat oil in wok; stir-fry pork, in batches, until cooked. Return pork to wok with sauce mixture, noodles and buk choy; stir-fry until buk choy is wilted.

preparation time 10 minutes
cooking time 10 minutes serves 4
nutritional count per serving
5.7g total fat (1.1g saturated fat); 1471kJ (352 cal);
31.6g carbohydrate; 39g protein; 2.9g fibre

pork and snake bean madras

4 rindless bacon rashers (260g), chopped finely
1 tablespoon peanut oil
700g pork fillet, sliced thinly
1 large white onion (200g), sliced thickly
¼ cup (75g) madras curry paste
200g snake (or green) beans, chopped coarsely
½ cup (125ml) beef stock
1 tablespoon tomato paste

1 Stir-fry bacon in heated wok until crisp; drain on absorbent paper.
2 Heat oil in wok; stir-fry pork and onion, in batches, until browned.
3 Stir-fry curry paste in wok until fragrant.
4 Add beans to wok with bacon, pork mixture, stock and paste; stir-fry, until sauce boils.

preparation time 10 minutes
cooking time 20 minutes serves 4
nutritional count per serving
23.4g total fat (6g saturated fat); 1986kJ (475 cal);
6g carbohydrate; 57.9g protein; 4.2g fibre

pork larb with broccolini

1 tablespoon peanut oil
2 cloves garlic, crushed
600g pork mince
⅓ cup (90g) grated palm sugar
2 tablespoons fish sauce
4 kaffir lime leaves, sliced finely
½ cup (40g) fried shallots
⅓ cup (45g) roasted unsalted peanuts
350g broccolini (or broccoli), trimmed,
    halved lengthways
1 tablespoon lime juice
1 cup loosely packed fresh coriander leaves
1 fresh long red chilli, sliced thinly
2 tablespoons coarsely chopped roasted
    unsalted peanuts

1 Heat oil in wok; stir-fry garlic and pork until pork is browned. Remove from wok.
2 Add sugar, sauce, lime leaves, shallots and nuts to wok; bring to the boil. Reduce heat; simmer, uncovered, 1 minute. Return pork to wok; cook, uncovered, about 2 minutes or until larb mixture is slightly dry and sticky.
3 Meanwhile, boil, steam or microwave broccolini; drain.
4 Stir juice and three-quarters of the coriander into larb off the heat; serve with broccolini, sprinkled with remaining coriander, chilli and coarsely chopped nuts.

preparation time 15 minutes
cooking time 10 minutes serves 4
nutritional count per serving
16g total fat (3g saturated fat); 1806kJ (432 cal);
25g carbohydrate; 44.1g protein; 5.5g fibre

pork kway teow

400g fresh rice noodles
1 tablespoon peanut oil
600g pork mince
1 medium brown onion (150g),
    sliced thinly
1 medium red capsicum (200g),
    sliced thinly
10cm stick fresh lemon grass (20g),
    chopped finely
2 tablespoons light soy sauce
¼ cup (60ml) lemon juice
1 tablespoon grated palm sugar
2 fresh small red thai chillies,
    chopped finely
1 cup coarsely chopped fresh coriander

1 Place noodles in large heatproof bowl, cover with boiling water; separate noodles with fork, drain.
2 Heat half the oil in wok; stir-fry pork until cooked through. Remove from wok.
3 Heat remaining oil in wok; stir-fry onion, capsicum and lemon grass until onion softens.
4 Return pork to wok with noodles, sauce, juice and sugar; stir-fry until hot. Stir in chilli and coriander.

preparation time 20 minutes
cooking time 10 minutes serves 4
nutritional count per serving
8.4g total fat (1.9g saturated fat); 1471kJ (352 cal);
29g carbohydrate; 38.8g protein; 1.5g fibre

singapore noodles

250g dried thin egg noodles
2 tablespoons peanut oil
4 eggs
1 tablespoon water
1 medium brown onion (150g),
    chopped finely
2 cloves garlic, crushed
2 tablespoons mild curry paste
200g pork mince
200g chinese barbecued pork, sliced thinly
200g cooked shelled small prawns
3 green onions, chopped coarsely
¼ cup (60ml) salt-reduced soy sauce
2 tablespoons oyster sauce
2 fresh small red thai chillies,
    chopped finely

1 Cook noodles in large saucepan of boiling water, uncovered, until just tender; drain.
2 Meanwhile, heat 2 teaspoons of the oil in wok; add half of the combined eggs and water, swirl wok to make thin omelette. Cook, uncovered, until egg is just set. Remove from wok; roll omelette, cut into thin strips. Heat another 2 teaspoons of the oil in wok; repeat process with remaining egg mixture.
3 Heat remaining oil in wok; stir-fry brown onion and garlic until onion softens. Add paste; stir-fry until fragrant. Add pork mince; stir-fry until changed in colour. Add barbecued pork, prawns, green onion, sauces, chilli and half of the omelette; stir-fry until hot. Add noodles; toss gently to combine, serve topped with remaining omelette.

preparation time 15 minutes
cooking time 10 minutes serves 4
nutritional count per serving
28.1g total fat (7.4g saturated fat); 2796kJ (669 cal);
51.5g carbohydrate; 47.8g protein; 5.1g fibre
tip Chinese barbecued pork can be bought from
Chinese food stores.

hot and spicy pork belly

You can also use 1.5kg pork belly rashers
or spare ribs.

1.5kg boneless pork belly
¾ cup (180ml) light soy sauce
1 egg
¼ cup (35g) plain flour
2 tablespoons vegetable oil
½ cup (125ml) rice wine
½ cup (100g) firmly packed brown sugar
¼ cup (50g) yellow mustard seeds
⅓ cup loosely packed, coarsely chopped
   fresh coriander
3 cloves garlic, crushed
5cm piece fresh ginger (25cm), grated
3 teaspoons dried chilli flakes
1 teaspoon five-spice powder
½ teaspoon cayenne pepper

1 Cut pork into individual rashers.
2 Place rashers in large saucepan. Cover
with water; bring to the boil. Reduce heat;
simmer, uncovered, about 10 minutes or
until rashers are almost cooked through.
Drain; pat dry with absorbent paper.
3 Blend ¼ cup (60ml) of the soy sauce with
the egg and flour in large bowl. Add rashers;
stir to coat in soy mixture.
4 Heat oil in wok; stir-fry rashers, in batches,
until browned all over.
5 Cook remaining soy sauce and remaining
ingredients in wok, stirring, until sugar
dissolves. Return rashers to wok; stir-fry
until heated through.

preparation time 10 minutes
cooking time 20 minutes serves 4
nutritional count per serving
13.4g total fat (2.4g saturated fat); 1785kJ (427 cal);
25.4g carbohydrate; 43.8g protein; 1g fibre

pork and hokkien noodle stir-fry

500g hokkien noodles
2 medium carrots (240g)
2 tablespoons peanut oil
1 medium brown onion (150g),
    sliced thickly
2 cloves garlic, crushed
300g broccoli, chopped coarsely
200g fresh baby corn, halved lengthways
600g pork stir-fry strips
1 teaspoon cornflour
1 tablespoon brown sugar
⅓ cup (80ml) sweet chilli sauce
2 tablespoons kecap manis

1 Place noodles in large heatproof bowl; cover with boiling water. Separate noodles with fork; drain.
2 Cut carrots into thin strips.
3 Heat half of the oil in wok; stir-fry onion and garlic until onion softens. Add carrot, broccoli and corn; stir-fry until just tender. Remove from wok.
4 Heat remaining oil in wok; stir-fry pork, in batches, until browned all over.
5 Blend cornflour and sugar with sauces in small jug. Return vegetables to wok with pork and sauce mixture; stir-fry until sauce boils and thickens slightly. Add noodles; stir-fry until heated through.

preparation time 15 minutes
cooking time 10 minutes serves 4
nutritional count per serving
12.5g total fat (2.3g saturated fat); 2266kJ (542 cal); 52.3g carbohydrate; 49g protein; 10.7g fibre

gingered pork with vegetables

700g pork fillet, sliced thinly
10cm piece fresh ginger (50g), grated
¼ cup coarsely chopped fresh coriander
2 tablespoons rice vinegar
2 tablespoons peanut oil
125g fresh baby corn, halved lengthways
1 medium red capsicum (200g),
    sliced thinly
100g snow peas, halved
2 tablespoons light soy sauce
250g spinach, trimmed
3 cups (240g) bean sprouts
½ cup loosely packed, fresh coriander
    leaves, extra

1 Combine pork in medium bowl with ginger, coriander and vinegar. Cover; refrigerate 3 hours or overnight.
2 Heat half of the oil in wok; stir-fry pork mixture, in batches, until pork is cooked through.
3 Heat remaining oil in wok. Stir-fry corn, capsicum and peas until just tender; remove from wok. Return pork to wok with soy sauce; stir-fry until hot. Return cooked vegetables to wok with spinach, sprouts and extra coriander; stir-fry until spinach just wilts.

preparation time 10 minutes (plus marinating time)
cooking time 15 minutes serves 4
nutritional count per serving
12.6g total fat (2.6g saturated fat); 1463kJ (350 cal); 10.3g carbohydrate; 45.9g protein; 5.7g fibre

curries & casseroles

sri lankan pork curry

2 tablespoons vegetable oil
20 fresh curry leaves
½ teaspoon fenugreek seeds
1 large brown onion (200g), chopped finely
4 cloves garlic, crushed
3cm piece fresh ginger (15g), grated
1 tablespoon curry powder
2 teaspoons cayenne pepper
1kg boneless pork belly, rind off,
   chopped coarsely
1 tablespoon white wine vinegar
2 tablespoons tamarind concentrate
1 cinnamon stick
4 cardamom pods, bruised
1½ cups (375ml) water
400ml can coconut milk

1 Heat half the oil in large saucepan; cook leaves and seeds until seeds pop and mixture is fragrant. Add onion, garlic and ginger; cook, stirring, until onion softens.
2 Stir in curry powder and cayenne, then pork. Add vinegar, tamarind, cinnamon, cardamom and the water; simmer, covered, 1 hour. Remove pork from pan.
3 Heat remaining oil in large frying pan. Cook pork, stirring, until browned.
4 Meanwhile, add coconut milk to curry sauce; simmer, stirring, about 5 minutes or until curry thickens slightly. Return pork to curry; stir until hot.

preparation time 20 minutes
cooking time 1 hour 20 minutes serves 4
nutritional count per serving
78.2g total fat (35.7g saturated fat); 3766kJ (901 cal);
8g carbohydrate; 42.1g protein; 3.6g fibre

oven-braised pork with fresh sage sauce

Ask the butcher to remove the rind from the rack. Rub the rind with a little oil, then with some sea salt flakes. Roast in a preheated oven (220°C/200°C fan-forced) until the rind crackles. Serve crackling as a snack or with the pork if you like.

90g butter
1kg rack of pork (6 cutlets)
2 medium carrots (240g), sliced thickly
6 baby brown onions (150g), peeled
4 cloves garlic, peeled
2 bay leaves
6 sprigs fresh thyme
1⅓ cups (330ml) dry white wine
fresh sage sauce
15g butter
1 tablespoon plain flour
2 tablespoons fresh sage leaves

1 Melt butter in large flameproof dish; cook pork until browned all over. Remove pork from dish. Cook carrot, onions, garlic, bay leaves and thyme in dish about 5 minutes or until vegetables are browned lightly.

2 Meanwhile, preheat oven to 180°C/160°C fan-forced.

3 Return pork to dish with wine; cook in oven, uncovered, about 1¼ hours or until pork is tender. Remove pork to heated plate; cover to keep warm.

4 Strain pan juices; discard vegetables.

5 Make fresh sage sauce.

6 Serve pork with sage sauce.

fresh sage sauce Bring reserved pan juices to the boil in small saucepan; whisk in blended butter and flour, whisking over heat until sauce boils and thickens slightly; stir in sage.

preparation time 15 minutes
cooking time 1 hour 30 minutes serves 6
nutritional count per serving
26.8g total fat (13.7g saturated fat); 1626kJ (389 cal);
4.9g carbohydrate; 23.1g protein; 1.7g fibre

maple-syrup-flavoured pork belly with pecans

1kg boneless pork belly, rind on
1 cup (250ml) pure maple syrup
3 cups (750ml) chicken stock
1 cinnamon stick
2 ancho chillies
6 cloves
2 cloves garlic, crushed
½ cup (125ml) light soy sauce
½ cup (125ml) orange juice
1 tablespoon olive oil
750g silver beet, trimmed, sliced thinly
½ cup (60g) coarsely chopped
    roasted pecans

1 Cut pork into four pieces. Combine pork, syrup, stock, cinnamon, chillies, cloves, garlic and soy sauce in large saucepan (pork should be in a single layer); bring to the boil. Reduce heat; simmer, covered, about 1½ hours or until pork is tender, turning pork every 30 minutes.
2 Remove pork; cover to keep warm. Stir juice into braising liquid; bring to the boil. Reduce heat; simmer, uncovered, about 5 minutes or until sauce thickens slightly. Strain sauce into small bowl.
3 Meanwhile, heat oil in large saucepan; cook silver beet, stirring, about 5 minutes or until wilted.
4 Cut each pork piece into quarters. Divide silver beet among plates; top with pork, drizzle with sauce then sprinkle with nuts.

preparation time 20 minutes
cooking time 1 hour 50 minutes serves 4
nutritional count per serving
67.2g total fat; 18.9g saturated fat; 4080kJ (976 cal); 62.3g carbohydrate; 34.7g protein; 4.1g fibre
tip Ancho chillies, the most commonly used chilli in Mexico, are poblano chillies which have been dried. Having a fruity, sweet and smoky flavour, they measure about 8cm in length and are dark reddish brown in colour.

pork red curry with green apple

¼ cup (60ml) peanut oil
600g pork fillet
¼ cup (75g) red curry paste
1 medium brown onion (150g),
    chopped coarsely
4cm piece fresh ginger (20g), grated
400ml can coconut milk
⅔ cup (160ml) chicken stock
3 medium green apples (450g)
½ cup (70g) roasted unsalted peanuts
½ cup coarsely chopped thai basil

1 Heat half the oil in large saucepan; cook pork, uncovered, until browned. Remove from pan, cover to keep warm.
2 Heat remaining oil in same pan; cook paste, onion and ginger, stirring, until onion softens. Add coconut milk and stock; bring to the boil. Reduce heat; simmer, uncovered, 5 minutes.
3 Meanwhile, peel, core and thinly slice apples. Return pork to pan with apple; simmer, covered, about 10 minutes or until apple softens. Remove from heat; remove pork, slice thickly.
4 Serve pork topped with curry mixture, sprinkled with nuts and basil.

preparation time 15 minutes
cooking time 20 minutes serves 4
nutritional count per serving
52.1g total fat (23.3g saturated fat); 3035kJ (726 cal); 18.5g carbohydrate; 43.5g protein; 7.3g fibre

apple, pork and prune casserole

2 tablespoons vegetable oil
2 small leeks (400g), sliced thinly
4 x 350g pork forequarter chops
¼ cup (35g) plain flour
1 litre (4 cups) chicken stock
½ cup (100g) long-grain white rice
4 medium apples (600g), sliced thickly
1 cup (170g) seeded prunes
2 tablespoons coarsely chopped
    fresh sage

1 Preheat oven to 180°C/160°C fan-forced.
2 Heat one-third of the oil in 2.5 litre (10-cup) flameproof casserole dish; cook leek, stirring, until soft. Remove from dish.
3 Trim fat and bone from chops; cut pork into 5cm pieces. Toss pork in flour; shake away excess flour.
4 Heat remaining oil in dish; cook pork, stirring, until browned. Add leek and stock to dish; cook, covered, in oven 45 minutes.
5 Remove dish from oven; skim off any fat. Stir in rice, apple, prunes and half of the sage; cook, covered, in oven about 20 minutes or until pork and rice are tender. Serve sprinkled with remaining sage.

preparation time 25 minutes
cooking time 1 hour 30 minutes serves 6
nutritional count per serving
23.6g total fat (6.7g saturated fat); 2082kJ (498 cal); 36.4g carbohydrate; 32.6g protein; 5.2g fibre

sweet and sour tamarind pork

2 tablespoons peanut oil
4 x 350g pork forequarter chops
1 tablespoon chinese cooking wine
1 cup (250ml) chicken stock
⅓ cup (80ml) tamarind concentrate
¼ cup (60ml) dark soy sauce
¼ cup (65g) grated palm sugar
1 medium red capsicum (200g),
  sliced thickly
1 medium green capsicum (200g),
  sliced thickly
1 medium red onion (170g), sliced thickly
3 green onions, sliced thickly
aromatic paste
4cm piece fresh galangal (20g),
  chopped finely
20cm stick fresh lemon grass (40g),
  chopped finely
2 cloves garlic, quartered
2 shallots (50g), chopped coarsely
1 tablespoon sambal oelek

1 Preheat oven to 150°C/130°C fan-forced.
2 Blend or process ingredients for aromatic paste until mixture becomes a coarse puree.
3 Heat half of the oil in large flameproof casserole dish; cook pork, in batches, until browned both sides.
4 Heat remaining oil in same dish; cook aromatic paste, stirring, until fragrant.
5 Return pork to dish with wine, stock, tamarind, soy, sugar, capsicums and red onion; bring to the boil. Cover; cook in oven 25 minutes, turning pork once halfway through cooking time.
6 Add green onion; cook, covered, in oven about 10 minutes or until green onion is tender. Serve with steamed rice, if desired.

....

preparation time 25 minutes
cooking time 50 minutes serves 4
nutritional count per serving
34.1g total fat (10.2g saturated fat); 2487kJ (595 cal); 25g carbohydrates; 45.8g protein; 2.4g fibre

pork with beans and beer

3 cloves garlic, crushed
½ teaspoon freshly ground black pepper
1.8kg pork scotch fillet
1 tablespoon olive oil
3 rindless bacon rashers (195g),
  chopped finely
2 medium brown onions (300g),
  sliced thinly
2 teaspoons caraway seeds
375ml can beer
1 cup (200g) dried haricot beans
1½ cups (375ml) chicken stock
¼ small (300g) white cabbage,
  shredded finely

1 Rub combined garlic and pepper all over pork. Secure pork with string at 2cm intervals to make an even shape.
2 Heat oil in 5 litre (20-cup) large flameproof casserole dish. Cook pork, turning, until browned all over. Remove from dish.
3 Cook bacon, onion and seeds in dish, stirring, until onion is soft and bacon browned lightly.
4 Return pork to dish. Add beer, beans and stock; simmer, covered, about 2 hours or until beans and pork are tender.
5 Remove pork from dish. Add cabbage; cook, stirring, until just wilted.

....

preparation time 20 minutes
cooking time 2 hours 20 minutes serves 8
nutritional count per serving
24.7g total fat (7.9g saturated fat); 2282kJ (546 cal); 14.3g carbohydrate; 60.1g protein; 6.7g fibre

chipotle pork belly with chorizo and smoked paprika

You can also use 1.5kg pork belly rashers or spare ribs.

4 chipotle chillies
1 cup (250ml) boiling water
1.5kg boneless pork belly
1 tablespoon olive oil
1 chorizo (170g), sliced thinly
2 medium red onions (340g),
    chopped coarsely
1 medium red capsicum (200g),
    chopped coarsely
1 medium green capsicum (200g),
    chopped coarsely
1 teaspoon smoked paprika
4 cloves garlic, crushed
3 x 400g cans crushed tomatoes
2 medium tomatoes (300g), chopped finely
½ cup finely chopped fresh coriander
2 teaspoons finely grated lime rind
1 clove garlic, crushed, extra

1 Preheat oven to 180°C/160°C fan-forced.
2 Soak chillies in the boiling water in small heatproof bowl for 10 minutes. Discard stalks from chillies; reserve chillies and liquid.
3 Cut pork into individual rashers. Heat oil in large deep flameproof casserole dish; cook rashers, in batches, until browned all over.
4 Cook chorizo, onion, capsicums, paprika and garlic in same dish, stirring, until onion softens. Return rashers to dish with undrained crushed tomatoes, chillies and reserved liquid. Cover; cook in oven about 1 hour.
5 Uncover; cook in oven about 1½ hours or until rashers are tender.
6 Meanwhile, combine chopped tomato, coriander, rind and extra garlic in small bowl.
7 Serve rashers topped with tomato mixture.

preparation time 20 minutes
cooking time 2 hours 50 minutes **serves** 6
nutritional count per serving
60.5g total fat (20g saturated fat); 3331kJ (797 cal); 13.4g carbohydrate; 48.8g protein; 5.2g fibre
tip Chipotle chillies, also known as ahumado, are jalapeño chillies that have been dried then smoked. They are about 6cm in length, a dark brown, almost black, colour and have a deep, intense smoky flavour rather than a blast of heat. They are available from herb and spice shops as well as many gourmet delicatessens.

pork.

Choosing the right cut from your supermarket or local butcher.

Pork Loin Cutlet Great individually on the barbecue or grilled as a whole rack.

Pork Loin Steaks Premium lean cut. Great for 4-minute steak.

Pork Loin Chop The classic Pork cut. Excellent on the barbecue or in a hotpot.

Diced Pork Versatile for a wide range of flavours. Use in curries, casseroles and stir-fries.

Minced Pork For spaghetti bolognaise, dim sum and san choy bau. Mixes excellently with other flavours and proteins, such as tofu.

Pork Rolled Loin (bone out) Premium roast with crackling. For an indulgent weekend roast.

Pork Belly Great cut into individual rashers or as a whole piece.

Pork Loin Rack For a visually impressive roast. With or without crackling.

Pork Mini Roast Perfect midweek roast for 3-4 people. Quick to cook.

pork and black-eyed beans

1 cup (200g) black-eyed beans
1kg pork scotch fillet, sliced thickly
⅓ cup (50g) plain flour
2 tablespoons olive oil
1 medium brown onion (150g),
    chopped coarsely
2 cloves garlic, crushed
½ teaspoon five-spice powder
1 teaspoon sichuan peppercorns,
    crushed coarsely
½ teaspoon chilli powder
½ cup (125ml) dry white wine
3 cups (750ml) chicken stock
2 teaspoons finely grated orange rind
½ cup coarsely chopped fresh
    flat-leaf parsley

1 Place beans in medium bowl, cover with cold water; stand overnight, drain. Rinse under cold water; drain.

2 Coat pork in flour, shake away excess. Heat half the oil in large flameproof casserole dish; cook pork, in batches, until browned all over.

3 Heat remaining oil in same dish; cook onion, garlic, five-spice, pepper and chilli, stirring, until fragrant. Add beans, wine and stock; bring to the boil.

4 Return pork to dish; simmer, covered, 40 minutes. Uncover; simmer about 30 minutes or until pork is tender and sauce thickens slightly, stirring occasionally. Remove from heat; stir in rind and parsley.

preparation time 20 minutes (plus standing time)
cooking time 1 hour 30 minutes **serves** 4
nutritional count per serving
19.9g total fat (5.1g saturated fat); 2608kJ (624 cal);
30.3g carbohydrate; 71.4g protein; 8.5g fibre
tip Also called black-eyed peas or cow peas, dried black-eyed beans are found in most supermarkets and large greengrocers alongside a wide range of other pulses, any of which can be substituted for what we've used here. Dried beans, peas, split peas and lentils are wise selections for the cook on a budget: not only are they cheap and filling, but are a good source of non-meat protein.

pork green curry

800g pork mince
3cm piece fresh ginger (15g), grated
1 fresh long red chilli, chopped finely
2 cloves garlic, crushed
⅓ cup coarsely chopped fresh coriander
1 tablespoon peanut oil
¼ cup (75g) green curry paste
2 x 400ml cans coconut milk
2 tablespoons lime juice
1 tablespoon fish sauce
1 tablespoon grated palm sugar
200g snake (or green) beans,
    cut into 5cm lengths
⅓ cup loosely packed thai basil leaves

1 Combine pork, ginger, chilli, garlic and
half the coriander in medium bowl; roll level
tablespoons of mixture into balls. Heat oil in
large frying pan; cook meatballs, in batches,
until browned.
2 Cook curry paste in same pan, stirring
until fragrant. Add coconut milk; bring to
the boil. Reduce heat; simmer, uncovered,
stirring occasionally, about 10 minutes.
3 Return meatballs to pan with juice,
sauce, sugar and beans; simmer, covered,
about 5 minutes or until meatballs are
cooked through.
4 Remove from heat; stir in remaining
coriander and basil.

preparation time 15 minutes
cooking time 25 minutes serves 4
nutritional count per serving
56.5g total fat (39.1g saturated fat); 3290kJ (787 cal);
13.7g carbohydrate; 53.8g protein; 7.3g fibre

sour pork curry

1 tablespoon vegetable oil
1kg pork scotch fillet
1 teaspoon shrimp paste
¼ cup coarsely chopped coriander root
    and stem mixture
2cm piece fresh galangal (10g),
    chopped finely
5 dried long red chillies, chopped finely
3 fresh long red chillies, chopped finely
2 tablespoons fish sauce
¾ cup (235g) tamarind concentrate
2 tablespoons white sugar
2 cups (500ml) chicken stock
1 litre (4 cups) water
½ cup fresh thai basil leaves,
    chopped coarsely

1 Heat oil in large flameproof casserole dish; cook pork, uncovered, until browned. Remove from dish.
2 Preheat oven to 160°C/140°C fan-forced.
3 Add paste, coriander mixture, galangal and chillies to same dish; cook, stirring, until fragrant. Add sauce, tamarind, sugar, stock and the water; bring to the boil. Return pork to dish, cover; cook in oven 1 hour. Uncover; cook 1 hour.
4 Remove pork from dish, cover; stand 10 minutes before slicing thickly. Stir basil into curry sauce off the heat.

preparation time 30 minutes
cooking time 2 hours 15 minutes serves 4
nutritional count per serving
9.3g total fat (2.1g saturated fat); 1680kJ (402 cal); 18.3g carbohydrate; 59.7g protein; 1.5g fibre

asian-style braised pork

1 tablespoon peanut oil
1kg pork scotch fillet
2 cinnamon sticks
2 star anise
½ cup (125ml) light soy sauce
½ cup (125ml) chinese rice wine
¼ cup (55g) firmly packed brown sugar
5cm piece fresh ginger (25g), sliced thinly
4 cloves garlic, quartered
1 medium brown onion (150g),
   chopped coarsely
1 cup (250ml) water

1 Preheat oven to 160°C/140°C fan-forced.
2 Heat oil in medium deep flameproof casserole dish; cook pork, until browned all over. Remove from heat.
3 Add combined spices, soy, wine, sugar, ginger, garlic, onion and the water to dish; turn pork to coat in mixture. Cook, uncovered, in oven about 2 hours or until pork is tender, turning every 20 minutes.
4 Remove pork; cover to keep warm. Strain braising liquid into medium saucepan; bring to the boil. Reduce heat; simmer, uncovered, 5 minutes or until sauce thickens slightly.
5 Serve pork drizzled with sauce.

preparation time 10 minutes
cooking time 2 hours 30 minutes serves 4
nutritional count per serving
24.7g total fat (7.6g saturated fat); 2274kJ (544 cal); 18.1g carbohydrate; 55.4g protein; 1.2g fibre

tamarind and citrus pork curry

70g dried tamarind, chopped coarsely
¾ cup (180ml) boiling water
1 tablespoon peanut oil
1 large red onion (300g), chopped finely
1 fresh long red chilli, sliced thinly
5cm piece fresh ginger (25g), grated
2 cloves garlic, crushed
10 fresh curry leaves
2 teaspoons fenugreek seeds
½ teaspoon ground turmeric
1 teaspoon ground coriander
1 teaspoon finely grated lime rind
1 tablespoon lime juice
400ml can coconut cream
6 baby eggplants (360g), chopped coarsely
1kg pork fillet, cut into 2cm dice

1 Soak tamarind in the boiling water for 30 minutes. Place fine sieve over small bowl; push tamarind through sieve. Discard solids in sieve; reserve pulp in bowl.

2 Heat oil in large saucepan; cook onion, chilli, ginger, garlic, curry leaves, seeds and spices, stirring, until onion softens.

3 Add tamarind pulp, rind, juice, coconut cream and eggplant; simmer, covered, 20 minutes. Add pork; simmer, uncovered, about 20 minutes or until pork is cooked.

preparation time 20 minutes (plus standing time)
cooking time 50 minutes serves 4
nutritional count per serving
29.8g total fat (20.2g saturated fat); 2529kJ (605 cal); 19.7g carbohydrate; 61.2g protein; 6.8g fibre

pork vindaloo

2 tablespoons ghee
1kg boneless shoulder of pork, diced
1 large red onion (300g), sliced thinly
½ cup (150g) vindaloo paste
2 cloves garlic, crushed
2 cups (500ml) water
¼ cup (60ml) white vinegar
4 medium potatoes (800g), quartered
2 fresh small red thai chillies,
   chopped finely
2 fresh long red chillies, sliced thinly

1 Heat ghee in large saucepan; cook pork, in batches, until browned all over.
2 Cook onion in same pan, stirring, until soft. Add paste and garlic; cook, stirring, about 1 minute or until fragrant.
3 Return pork to pan with the water and vinegar; simmer, covered, 50 minutes.
4 Add potato; simmer, uncovered, about 45 minutes or until potato is tender. Stir in chopped chilli; serve curry sprinkled with thinly sliced chilli.

preparation time 25 minutes
cooking time 1 hour 50 minutes serves 4
nutritional count per serving
40.7g total fat (13.7g saturated fat); 3173kJ (759 cal); 33.3g carbohydrate; 61g protein; 8.3g fibre

pork ragu with pappardelle

2 x 5cm-thick pork scotch fillet (750g)
2 tablespoons plain flour
1 tablespoon olive oil
20g butter
1 medium leek (350g), sliced
3 cloves garlic, sliced
1 medium fennel bulb (200g), sliced thinly,
   reserve fennel tops
½ cup (125ml) dry white wine
1½ cups (375ml) chicken stock
500g pappardelle pasta
2 teaspoons balsamic vinegar
½ cup (80g) seeded green olives

1 Preheat oven to 160°C/140°C fan-forced.
2 Toss pork in flour; shake away excess. Heat oil and butter in flameproof casserole dish; add pork, cook until browned all over.
3 Add leek, garlic and fennel to dish; stir over medium heat until softened. Add wine; bring to the boil. Reduce heat; simmer, uncovered, until wine is almost evaporated. Add stock; bring to the boil.
4 Cover dish; cook in oven for about 2 hours or until pork is tender, turning halfway.
5 Cool pork 10 minutes, then tear into small pieces.
6 Meanwhile, cook pasta in large saucepan of boiling water, uncovered, until tender; drain. Return to pan.
7 Reheat the pork and sauce, stir in vinegar and olives. Add pork and sauce to pasta, toss gently to combine. Serve sprinkled with reserved fennel tops.

preparation time 25 minutes
cooking time 2 hours 10 minutes serves 6
nutritional count per serving
12g total fat (4.2g saturated fat); 2274kJ (544 cal); 62.8g carbohydrate; 39.3g protein; 5.3g fibre

panang pork curry with pickled snake beans

2¾ cups (680ml) coconut milk
3⅓ cups (830ml) water
1.5kg boneless shoulder of pork, diced
1⅔ cups (410ml) coconut cream
¼ cup (65g) grated palm sugar
¼ cup (60ml) fish sauce
6 kaffir lime leaves, sliced thinly
190g can sliced bamboo shoots, drained
⅓ cup coarsely chopped fresh thai basil
¼ cup coarsely chopped fresh coriander
2 fresh long red chillies, sliced thinly

pickled snake beans
350g snake (or green) beans, trimmed
1 cup (250ml) water
1 cup (250ml) white vinegar
1 tablespoon malt vinegar
1 cup (220g) white sugar
2 tablespoons coarse cooking salt

panang paste
6 fresh long red chillies, chopped coarsely
3 cloves garlic, peeled, quartered
2 thai purple shallots, chopped coarsely
2 teaspoons coarsely chopped
  coriander root
2 tablespoons finely chopped
  fresh galangal
10cm stick fresh lemon grass (20g),
  chopped finely
¼ cup (60ml) water
½ cup (75g) roasted unsalted peanuts

1 Make pickled snake beans.
2 Make panang paste. Measure ⅓ cup of the paste for this recipe, then freeze the rest.
3 Combine half of the coconut milk and the water in medium saucepan; bring to the boil. Add pork; bring to the boil. Reduce heat; simmer, uncovered, about 1 hour or until tender. Remove pan from heat; cool pork in liquid 30 minutes.
4 Heat coconut cream in large saucepan for about 10 minutes or until fat separates from cream. Add the ⅓ cup panang paste; cook, stirring, 10 minutes. Stir palm sugar and fish sauce into mixture; add 1 cup pork cooking liquid (discard any that remains). Stir in remaining coconut milk, lime leaves, bamboo shoots and drained pork; simmer, uncovered, until heated through.
5 Serve curry sprinkled with basil, coriander and chilli. Serve with pickled snake beans.

pickled snake beans Cut beans into 5cm lengths; place in medium heatproof bowl. Combine the water, vinegars, sugar and salt in small saucepan; stir over heat until sugar dissolves. Bring to the boil, remove from heat; cool 10 minutes, pour over beans. Refrigerate beans, covered, 3 hours or overnight.

panang paste Blend chilli, garlic, shallot, coriander, galangal, lemon grass and the water until smooth; add nuts, pulse until combined.

preparation time 30 minutes (plus cooling and refrigeration times)
cooking time 1 hour 30 minutes serves 6
nutritional count per serving
50.8g total fat (36.9g saturated fat); 3954kJ (946 cal); 56.7g carbohydrate; 62.9g protein; 6.1g fibre

braised pork with fennel

Ask the butcher to roll and tie the pork shoulder for you.

2 tablespoons olive oil

1.5kg boneless rolled shoulder of pork, rind off

2 cloves garlic, crushed

1 medium brown onion (150g), chopped coarsely

½ small fennel bulb (100g), chopped coarsely

8 slices hot pancetta (120g), chopped coarsely

1 tablespoon tomato paste

½ cup (125ml) dry white wine

400g can crushed tomatoes

1 cup (250ml) chicken stock

1 cup (250ml) water

2 sprigs fresh rosemary

2 large fennel bulbs (1kg), halved, sliced thickly

spice rub

1 teaspoon fennel seeds

2 teaspoons dried oregano

½ teaspoon cayenne pepper

1 tablespoon cracked black pepper

1 tablespoon sea salt flakes

2 teaspoons olive oil

1 Preheat oven to 180°C/160°C fan-forced.

2 Heat oil in large flameproof casserole dish; cook pork until browned all over.

3 Meanwhile, combine ingredients for spice rub in small bowl.

4 Remove pork from dish; discard all but 1 tablespoon of the oil in dish. Cook garlic, onion, chopped fennel and pancetta in same dish, stirring, until onion softens. Add paste; cook, stirring, 2 minutes.

5 Meanwhile, rub pork with spice rub.

6 Return pork to dish with wine, undrained tomatoes, stock, the water and rosemary; bring to the boil. Cover; cook in oven 1 hour.

7 Add sliced fennel; cook, covered, in oven 1 hour. Remove pork from dish; discard rind. Cover to keep warm.

8 Meanwhile, cook braising liquid in dish over medium heat, uncovered, until thickened slightly. Return sliced pork to dish; serve pork with sauce.

preparation time 25 minutes
cooking time 2 hours 50 minutes serves 6
nutritional count per serving
32.8g total fat (10.7g saturated fat); 2525kJ (604 cal); 7.5g carbohydrate; 66.5g protein; 4.6g fibre

glossary

ALLSPICE also known as pimento or jamaican pepper; available whole or ground. Tastes like a blend of cinnamon, clove and nutmeg.

BEANS
black-eyed also known as black-eyed peas or cowpea; the dried seed of a variant of the snake or yard-long bean. Not dissimilar to white beans in flavour; good cooked and used cold in salads.
snake long (about 40cm), thin, round, fresh green beans, Asian in origin, with a taste similar to green or french beans. Used most frequently in stir-fries, they are also known as yard-long beans because of their length.
white in this book, some recipes may simply call for "white beans", a generic term we use for canned or dried cannellini, haricot, navy or great northern beans which are all of the same family, *phaseolus vulgaris*.

BROCCOLINI a cross between broccoli and Chinese kale; long asparagus-like stems with a long loose floret, both completely edible. Resembles broccoli, but is milder and sweeter in taste.

BUK CHOY also known as bok choy, pak choi, chinese white cabbage or chinese chard; has a fresh, mild mustard taste. Use both stems and leaves. Baby buk choy is smaller and more tender.

CARAWAY SEEDS the small, half-moon-shaped dried seed from a member of the parsley family; adds a sharp anise flavour in sweet and savoury dishes.

CARDAMOM can be purchased in pod, seed or ground form. Has a distinctive aromatic, sweetly rich flavour, and is one of the world's most expensive spices.

CAYENNE PEPPER a thin-fleshed, long, extremely hot, dried red chilli, usually purchased ground.

FENNEL also known as finocchio or anise; a crunchy green vegetable slightly resembling celery that's eaten raw in salads; fried as an accompaniment; or used as an ingredient in soups and sauces. Also sometimes the name given to the dried seeds of the plant which have a stronger licorice flavour.

FIVE-SPICE POWDER ingredients vary, but usually consists of ground cloves, cinnamon, star anise, sichuan pepper and fennel seeds. Available at most supermarkets or Asian food shops.

FRIED SHALLOTS used as a condiment, sprinkled over just-cooked food. Found in cellophane bags or jars at Asian food shops; once opened, they will keep for months if stored tightly sealed. Make your own by frying thinly sliced peeled shallots until golden brown and crisp.

GALANGAL also known as ka or lengkaus if fresh and laos if dried and powdered; a root similar to ginger in its use. Having a hot, sour ginger-citrusy flavour; used in fish curries and soups.

HOISIN SAUCE a thick, sweet and spicy Chinese barbecue sauce made from salted fermented soybeans, onions and garlic. Available from Asian food shops and supermarkets.

JAPANESE SOY SAUCE an all-purpose low-sodium soy sauce made with more wheat content than Chinese varieties; fermented in barrels and aged. Possibly the best table soy and the one to choose if you only want one variety.

KAFFIR LIME LEAVES also known as bai magrood, looks like two glossy dark green leaves joined end to end, forming a rounded hourglass shape. Used fresh or dried, they are used like bay leaves or curry leaves, especially in Thai cooking. Sold fresh, dried or frozen, the dried leaves are less potent so double the number if using them as a substitute for fresh; a strip of fresh lime peel may be substituted for each leaf.

KIPFLER POTATO small, finger-shaped, nutty flavour; great baked and in salads.

LEMON GRASS also known as takrai, serai or serah. A tall, clumping, lemon-smelling and tasting, sharp-edged aromatic tropical grass; the white lower part of the stem is used, finely chopped. Can be found, fresh, dried, powdered and frozen, in supermarkets, greengrocers and Asian food shops.

MAPLE SYRUP distilled from the sap of maple trees found only in Canada and parts of North America. Maple-flavoured syrup or pancake syrup is not an adequate substitute for the real thing.

MIRIN a Japanese champagne-coloured cooking wine, made of glutinous rice and alcohol. It is used expressly for cooking and should not be confused with sake.

MIZUNA frizzy Japanese green salad leaves with a delicate mustard flavour.

PALM SUGAR also known as nam tan pip, jaggery, jawa or gula melaka; made from the sap of the sugar palm tree. Light brown to black in colour and usually sold in rock-hard cakes; use brown sugar if unavailable.

PANCETTA an Italian unsmoked bacon, pork belly cured in salt and spices then rolled into a sausage shape and dried for several weeks. Used, sliced or chopped, as an ingredient rather than eaten on its own.

PROSCIUTTO a kind of unsmoked Italian ham; salted, air-cured and aged, it is usually eaten uncooked.

RADICCHIO Italian in origin; a member of the chicory family. The dark burgundy leaves and strong, bitter flavour can be cooked or eaten raw in salads.

SAMBAL OELEK also ulek or olek; Indonesian in origin, is a salty paste made from ground chillies and vinegar.

SHIITAKE MUSHROOMS fresh, they're also known as Chinese black, forest or golden oak mushrooms. Although cultivated, they have the earthiness and taste of wild mushrooms and are large and meaty. Dried shiitakes are also called donko or dried Chinese mushrooms and have a unique meaty flavour. Rehydrate before use.

STAR ANISE a dried star-shaped pod whose seeds have an astringent aniseed flavour; commonly used to flavour stocks and marinades.

TAMARIND the tamarind tree produces clusters of hairy brown pods, each of which is filled with seeds and a viscous pulp, that are dried and pressed into the blocks of tamarind found in Asian food shops. Gives a sweet-sour, slightly astringent taste.

THAI BASIL also known as horapa; different from holy basil and sweet basil in both look and taste, having smaller leaves and purplish stems. It has a slight aniseed taste.

THAI EGGPLANT found in a variety of different sizes and colours, from a long, thin, purplish-green one to a hard, round, golf-ball size having a white-streaked pale-green skin.

WASABI an Asian horseradish used to make the pungent, green-coloured sauce traditionally served with Japanese raw fish dishes; sold in powdered or paste form.

WOMBOK also known as chinese cabbage, peking or napa cabbage; elongated in shape with pale green, crinkly leaves, is the most common cabbage in South East Asia. Can be shredded or chopped and eaten raw or braised, steamed or stir-fried.

conversion chart

MEASURES

One Australian metric measuring cup holds approximately 250ml; one Australian metric tablespoon holds 20ml; one Australian metric teaspoon holds 5ml.

The difference between one country's measuring cups and another's is within a two- or three-teaspoon variance, and will not affect your cooking results. North America, New Zealand and the United Kingdom use a 15ml tablespoon.

All cup and spoon measurements are level. The most accurate way of measuring dry ingredients is to weigh them. When measuring liquids, use a clear glass or plastic jug with the metric markings.

We use large eggs with an average weight of 60g.

DRY MEASURES

METRIC	IMPERIAL
15g	½oz
30g	1oz
60g	2oz
90g	3oz
125g	4oz (¼lb)
155g	5oz
185g	6oz
220g	7oz
250g	8oz (½lb)
280g	9oz
315g	10oz
345g	11oz
375g	12oz (¾lb)
410g	13oz
440g	14oz
470g	15oz
500g	16oz (1lb)
750g	24oz (1½lb)
1kg	32oz (2lb)

LIQUID MEASURES

METRIC	IMPERIAL
30ml	1 fluid oz
60ml	2 fluid oz
100ml	3 fluid oz
125ml	4 fluid oz
150ml	5 fluid oz (¼ pint/1 gill)
190ml	6 fluid oz
250ml	8 fluid oz
300ml	10 fluid oz (½ pint)
500ml	16 fluid oz
600ml	20 fluid oz (1 pint)
1000ml (1 litre)	1¾ pints

LENGTH MEASURES

METRIC	IMPERIAL
3mm	⅛in
6mm	¼in
1cm	½in
2cm	¾in
2.5cm	1in
5cm	2in
6cm	2½in
8cm	3in
10cm	4in
13cm	5in
15cm	6in
18cm	7in
20cm	8in
23cm	9in
25cm	10in
28cm	11in
30cm	12in (1ft)

OVEN TEMPERATURES

These oven temperatures are only a guide for conventional ovens. For fan-forced ovens, check the manufacturer's manual.

	°C (CELSIUS)	°F (FAHRENHEIT)	GAS MARK
Very slow	120	250	½
Slow	150	275-300	1-2
Moderately slow	160	325	3
Moderate	180	350-375	4-5
Moderately hot	200	400	6
Hot	220	425-450	7-8
Very hot	240	475	9

index

118

The delicious truth about
pork.

False Pork is difficult to cook.

True Pork is fast and easy to cook. Try a 4-minute steak – sizzle your steak on medium heat for 2 minutes. Turn once. Sizzle the other side for 2 minutes. Remove from pan and rest for 1 minute. Serve and enjoy the juicy flavour!

False Pork is strictly for Sunday roast.

True Pork is an amazingly versatile meat, perfect for barbecues and quick steaks as well as stir-fries, meatballs, kebabs, tortillas, dumplings. The opportunities are endless!

False Pork does not go well with different sauces.

True Pork goes fantastically well with a huge range of flavours and cooking styles! Pork goes perfectly with sauces like plum, soy, oyster, chilli, English mustard and ginger.

False You have to cook Pork right through.

True "If the truth be told, it's never been necessary with Australian Pork. Our farmers use the safest most advanced techniques, which means our Pork is of the highest standard." Dr Dean Gutzke PhD, Food Science and Technology.

False Pork is dry and tasteless.

True Pork is at its juicy, succulent best when cooked with a hint of pink in the middle. Pork can dry out when overcooked – so remember, if you want to enjoy your Pork juicy and tender, less is more!

False Pork is a fatty meat.

True Many Pork cuts are actually lean. In fact, there are 15 cuts approved by the Heart Foundation.

easy peasy **Pork** Juicy Tender